# DERAILING THE TOKYO EXPRESS

# Derailing the Tokyo Express

## The Naval Battles for the Solomon Islands That Sealed Japan's Fate

### Jack D. Coombe

Stackpole Books

Published by
STACKPOLE BOOKS
Cameron and Kelker Streets
P.O. Box 1831
Harrisburg, PA 17105

*All photos courtesy U.S. Naval Institute, Annapolis*
*Maps by Uzal W. Ent*
*Cover design by Caroline Miller*

Printed in the United States of America

First Edition

10 9 8 7 6 5 4 3 2 1

**Library of Congress Cataloging-in-Publication Data**

Coombe, Jack D.
    Derailing the Tokyo Express : the naval battles for the Solomon
Islands that sealed Japan's fate / Jack D. Coombe. — 1st ed.
        p.    cm.
    Includes bibliographical references and index.
    ISBN 0-8117-3030-1
    1. World War, 1939–1945 — Campaigns — Solomon Islands.  1. Title.
D767.98.C65    1991
940.54′26 — dc20                                                      91-7799
                                                                          CIP

*To the brave men and officers
of the destroyers of the U.S.
Pacific Fleet who, outgunned
and outnumbered, bore the brunt
of the savage battles with the
Tokyo Express during the
Solomon Islands campaign.*

# Contents

# Preface

This book is the result of forty-four years of study, meditation, and note-taking initiated since World War II. It is a book I've always wanted to write but somehow never got underway until my agent, Gerry Wallerstein, approached me on behalf of Stackpole Books, and I decided to press forward with my long-simmering project.

Having participated in the entire Pacific War, from 1941 to 1945, and having taken part in many of the naval campaigns, I consider the struggle for the Solomons to be the epitome of the fighting at sea during World War II. Those battles, some fought at almost point-blank range, signaled the end of the classic surface fighting, with the possible exception of a short engagement in the Philippines in 1944. But that encounter was more of a skirmish than an engagement between fleet of ships, such as those that took place in the Solomons from late 1942 to early 1943.

During my research, a thesis I'd been developing for many years became clear to me. The thesis was that the struggle for the Solomon Islands, and not the Battle of Midway, was the turning point in the war for Japan. After Midway, the Imperial fleet was still more powerful than ours and could have easily defeated the U.S. fleet in a decisive engagement. It was not until they were driven out of the Solomons that the Japanese began to lose the war. It is my intention to prove that thesis in this book.

The American landings on Guadalcanal in August 1942 were designed to dislodge the occupying Japanese forces there. Those landings provoked a swift and deadly response from Imperial General Headquarters. Fierce air and sea attacks were made with the object of driving U.S. forces from the entire region. When these attacks failed, it became obvious that Imperial forces had to be reinforced. Thus the Tokyo Express was born.

The Tokyo Express consisted of mainline fleet destroyers and cruisers, the pride of the Imperial Navy. Its purpose was to reinforce the beleaguered troops on Guadalcanal and to beef up garrisons on Bougainville, New Georgia, and Choiseul islands, among others. Against these forces, the Americans fielded a handful of old destroyers and, in some cases, cruisers. Fierce encounters sometimes took place at point-blank range. Although U.S. warships were fine vessels with brave and skilled crews, they were poorly matched against the enemy's splendid, newer ships and highly disciplined crews. The term "Tokyo Express" was given these forces, as far as I have determined, merely because of their train-like regularity.

Many sources were tapped during the months of research and were coupled with my own memoirs and reminiscences. Guadalcanal, the Slot, Iron Bottom Sound, and New Guinea were spots upon which I walked, or sailed, during those early, dark days of World War II.

Most of the technical research, of course, was done at the U.S. Navy's historical center in Washington, D.C.; I consulted privately printed sources and the personal reminiscences of participants.

Many of the conversations in the work are actual, having been heard or participated in on the bridges of U.S. warships. Others, such as those on Japanese warships, are conjectural, carefully reconstructed through intensive research and from some recorded conversations in Japanese accounts. I believe these discussions are as close as possible to those that actually took place.

This work is as accurate and up-to-date as research will allow, but my goal has been to faithfully relate a whopping good war story. I trust that I have done just that.

# Acknowledgments

I offer my grateful thanks to those who contributed to this book. I am particularly indebted to Mr. Bernard F. Cavalcante and his excellent staff of the Operational Archives Branch of the Naval Historical Center in Washington, D.C. Special thanks go to Mike Walker, archivist specialist, who gave invaluable assistance during my research stay in that city by suggesting sources about which I otherwise would not have known.

Among those who generously offered their help with information were Tom Elliott, William C. Croft, F. A. Gingros, Robert B. Hirth, Earl Hughes, Ed Krammen, Jim Mincey, Bob Murkey, Donald C. Sinclair, Capt. John B. Tazewell, USN, and Bernard J. Press.

My agent, Gerry B. Wallerstein, gave me advice and encouragement beyond the usual business-like communications between agent and client, by being a friend and adviser.

Much gratitude to my editor, Mary Suggs, and her able assistant, Ann Wagoner, of Stackpole Books for their patient work with me in the writing and preparation of the manuscript.

An appreciative nod goes to Mrs. Virginia Fender, periodicals librarian, Glenview Public Library, Glenview, Illinois, for her thoughtful help in the Herculean task of copying materials from many reels of microfilm.

Finally, my heartfelt gratitude to my wife, Peg, for becoming an "author's widow" during the months of research and writing and, of course, for her never-ending encouragement and support.

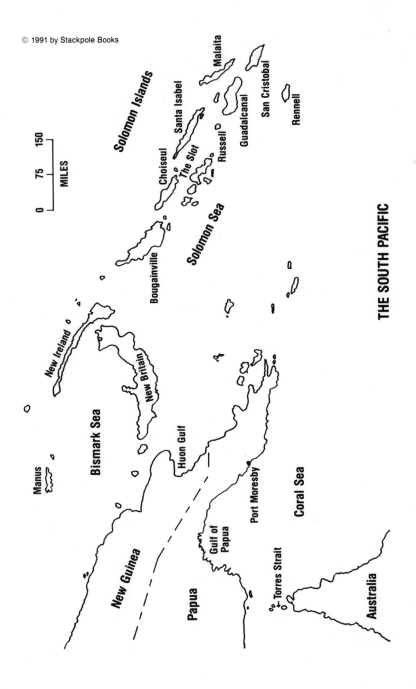

Solomon Islands

Malaita

Santa Isabel

San Cristobal

Choiseul

The Slot

Russell

Guadalcanal

Rennell

MILES

150

75

0

Solomon Sea

Bougainville

New Ireland

New Britain

Manus

Bismark Sea

Huon Gulf

New Guinea

Papua

Gulf of Papua

Port Moresby

Coral Sea

Torres Strait

Australia

THE SOUTH PACIFIC

# 1
# Preliminary Bouts

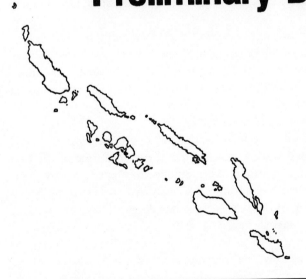

The crushing defeat of the U.S. Navy at Pearl Harbor on December 7, 1941, offered two shocks to the world. One was that the Japanese had the audacity and logistical means to thrust a large, powerful carrier force a staggering 3,400 miles across the Pacific, refueling along the way, and then strike at the U.S. fleet and return to Japan without losing a ship.

The other was the shattering of the myth of Japan's "paper navy." Though it was known that Japan had a sizable fleet, the prevailing impression among us navy men at the time was that the Imperial Navy was inferior to ours. The feeling was strengthened by purposeful visits to Western ports by Japan's decrepit training ships, which gave the impression of a third-rate fleet that was no match for the "modern" navies of the United States and Britain. The charade succeeded moderately.

I remember leaning over the stern rail of the destroyer *Patterson* at a port in early 1941, chatting with a shipmate.

"Do you think we'll go to war with Japan?" I asked.

"Mebbe," he replied. "But I hear if we do, we'll sink their navy in six months."

Such was the feeling of many sailors in the Pacific Fleet in those days!

What a shock to later realize that Japan had a modern fleet of battleships, carriers, cruisers, and destroyers! Those fine ships were under the command of Fleet Admiral Isoruku Yamamoto, the Imperial Navy's most brilliant tactician. His attack on Pearl Harbor swept away all delusions about the Imperial Navy. It had proven to be bold, daring, and awesomely powerful.

The warlords, for their part, were not surprised at the Pearl Harbor success and were confident that the entire Pacific would soon be under their domination. This attitude arose from "victory fever" among the Japanese high command. And why not? Hadn't the "invincible" fleet crippled the U.S. Navy in one decisive blow? The spirit of *kodo-ha*, "the imperial way," was rampant among the top Japanese militarists.

Without pausing, the Japanese launched a bold series of strikes and landings across Southeast Asia and the eastern Pacific to consolidate their "Greater East Asia Co-Prosperity Sphere." One by one fell the Philippines, Singapore, Borneo, Indonesia, Hong Kong, and Burma. Victory was spearheaded by *Rengo Kantai*, the magnificent, undefeated Combined Fleet.

Not satisfied with all this real estate, Tokyo strategists cast covetous eyes southeastward to the Solomons, that "dagger" of islands aimed straight at Australia. In a lightning-like thrust, Imperial forces occupied Rabaul on New Britain, the handle of the dagger, with its vast Simpson Harbor, to use as a staging area for movements toward Tulagi and Guadalcanal. It was a bold plan that would take many ships, planes, and men, but first a base close to Australia had to be secured. Port Moresby on the Papuan Peninsula of New Guinea was decided upon.

In May 1942, an invasion group entered the Coral Sea, bound for Port Moresby. This powerful Japanese task force included troop transports protected by three carriers and screening vessels.

But the Americans had been tipped off to the movement and Adm. Frank Jack Fletcher was there to meet it with two carriers. During the confused battle that followed, the Japanese lost the light carrier *Shoho* and another carrier was damaged; the Americans lost the fleet carrier *Lexington*, a tanker, and a destroyer. Despite the losses, the United States had turned back the invasion force and Port Moresby was safe for the time being.

At Combined Fleet headquarters, Admiral Yamamoto fussed for a time, then dismissed the Coral Sea, turning his attention to a problem that had tormented him for some time: the absence of the American carriers at Pearl Harbor. It was a sword hanging over his head.

The stolid, grim-faced admiral had told headquarters that in the final analysis, Japan's entire strategy in the Pacific would depend on whether he could destroy the American fleet, especially its carrier task forces. He wanted a decisive fleet-to-fleet battle that would knock out American sea power and allow his Combined Fleet to roam at will across the Pacific.

Thus, in late April aboard the superbattleship *Yamato* in the secluded, warship-filled Hasharajima anchorage, the admiral and his staff put the finishing touches on a plan he'd been nurturing for months and that the recent Doolittle B-25 bomber raid on Tokyo had finally solidified. He studied the map of the Pacific intently. Then he jabbed a finger at a spot 1,136 miles northwest of Hawaii, turned to his staff and said, "There lies Midway Island, our objective. It will make a strategic base from which to bomb Hawaii into submission and force the American fleet out to challenge us. We will fight a decisive battle in which we will destroy it."

His awed staff listened to the requirements: more than 150 warships, support vessels, and transports loaded with 5,000 troops. A second carrier force would attack the Aleutians in an attempt to lure American forces there.

He was pleased; it was a perfect plan and he had the overwhelming strength to take Midway and destroy the U.S. Navy. He didn't know that there already were two strikes against his plan: his code had been broken by the U.S. Navy and three U.S. carriers would be there to meet him.[1]

After Adm. Chester Nimitz, commander in chief of the Pacific Fleet, learned of the plan, he dispatched two task forces to Midway: No. 16, with Adm. Raymond A. Spruance in command with the carrier *Yorktown*; and No. 17, under command of Admiral Fletcher, with the carriers *Enterprise* and *Hornet*. It wasn't much, considering Yamamoto's strength, but it was all that could be mustered.

The task forces reached "Point Luck," the rendezvous 350 miles northwest of Midway, on June 4. There, the forces slowed and began a classic zigzag pattern, awaiting further intelligence on Yamamoto's movements.[2]

The suspense was unbearable, for everyone knew that they were up against a superior force. As one gunner's mate remarked, "It looks like we'll fight the whole damn Nip navy here!" But everyone vowed to make the enemy pay dearly for any victory over us.

The Pacific was as blue as ever off Midway that day. The sky almost matched it, and only a few puffs of clouds drifted by. Seeing the ships move along, it seemed incredible that a battle to the death was at hand. Most of us slept at our guns at night, and all felt a sense of dread, tempered by confidence in our ships and airmen, who all believed would clip the wings of the Imperial Navy.

All hands were amazed to see the *Yorktown*. They knew that she had been badly damaged in the Coral Sea. The old girl had been quite a sight, battered but proud, limping into dry dock at the Pearl Harbor Navy Yard. An army of workers had labored day and night to put her into shape for the battle. And there she was, in all her glory, plowing along in the blue waters of Point Luck!

Suddenly, from TBS (talk between ships) came a chilling report: "Midway is under attack! I repeat, Midway is under attack!" It turned everyone's blood cold; the fat was in the fire. The carriers turned into the wind and launched air patrols to search for the enemy.

It's always thrilling to see planes rolling off a carrier deck like cliff swallows darting out of their holes and gliding gracefully along the air currents. Despite the possibility that some wouldn't return, all hands cheered their heads off. Let Yamamoto get a taste of that!

Later we learned that Midway had been badly damaged, but three enemy carriers had been set on fire and were sinking. Losses among American planes and men were heavy. Then everyone held his breath when it was revealed that one Japanese carrier had not been located. That ship, the *Hiryu*, had launched planes that would soon mortally wound the *Yorktown*. General quarters had been sounded, guns manned, and planed launched. This was to be it!

We knew we were in for it. It was to be our first air attack on the open ocean (the attack on Pearl Harbor occurred within an enclosed space), and all hands were apprehensive but alert. The *Yorktown* was still launching planes

Then TBS squawked: "Prepare to repel enemy air attack!"

Gunfire to the southwest alerted the fleet that the enemy had arrived. The destroyer pickets and carrier fighters had downed some of the enemy planes, but a few got through and attacked. The *Yorktown* was targeted, probably because she was nearest the attack point.

Words can't express the fury of an air attack. The sky is filled with aircraft desperately dodging innumerable puffs of exploding anti-aircraft shells. Gunners keep firing, hoping to hit one of those dreaded planes. In spite of the danger, fear gives away to numbness and one acts as if in a trance, squeezing the trigger until fingers ache and hands freeze in position, even after the ammunition runs out.

When the attack ends, fear takes over again and one shakes and sweats, thankful to be alive. It was not shameful for many to foul their skivvies at times like that.

We had faith in our commander, fifty-six-year-old Admiral Fletcher. We knew that the intense, athletic, and firm-jawed officer was up to the task. But the Japanese attack was too fierce and made with too much resolve. His beloved *Yorktown* had taken serious hits. The gallant carrier was burning and listing, but she was still afloat.

The big carrier had been hit by torpedoes on her port side that tore huge holes and wracked her with internal explosions. She ran in wild circles, listing badly, while her helpless screening ships stood by. The captain gave orders to abandon ship.

Remarkably, the carrier remained afloat. Maybe there was a chance to save her. A navy tug *Vireo* came alongside, ran a line to her and, assisted by the destroyers *Gwin* and *Monaghan*, attempted to tow her back to Pearl Harbor with salvage and fire-fighting crews aboard. Then the destroyer *Hammann* was ordered alongside to assist. For a time, it looked as if the old girl might be saved after all.

Unknown to all, the Japanese submarine I-168 was shadowing this activity, with intentions to kill when the opportunity arose. The *Hammann*'s going alongside gave her that chance. She fired four torpedoes. Two of the "fish" smashed into the *Yorktown*'s starboard side. Another hit the *Hammann*. The hapless destroyer broke in two and slipped beneath the waves in four minutes.

Five screening destroyers raced out, looking for the sub. Sonar contacts were made and depth charges were dropped, but the I-168 slipped away unharmed.[3]

Despite her mortal wounds, the *Yorktown* stayed afloat overnight. When dawn broke, she rolled over and went down. There were many tears in the eyes of crews nearby; the "Big Y" was a popular ship. It was ironic that she had been mauled in the Coral Sea, and then patched up in record time, only to be sunk at Midway.

The battle of Midway dealt the Imperial Navy a disastrous defeat. Fleet carriers *Kaga, Akagi, Hiryu,* and *Soryu*, part of the original Pearl Harbor strike force, had been sunk.[4] Although it was a staggering blow to the Japanese, American losses were ominous; our Pacific carrier strength had been pared from four to three, a loss not to be taken lightly.

Many have said that the loss of four Japanese fleet carriers was the turning point of the war. It is true and false: true in that a huge bite had been taken from the Combined Fleet, false in that Yamamoto's surface fleet was still twice the size of the Americans'. He still had six carriers, with more building. Essentially, then, the Japanese Navy was still as dangerous as ever. Midway merely slowed it down and put it on the defensive. Yamamoto's navy was still the most powerful force in the Pacific. With this confidence, the warlords once more turned their attention to the South Pacific and the Solomon Islands.

The Solomon Islands.

To a generation of Americans brought up on Dorothy Lamour and Jon Hall movies, any island in the Pacific was a paradise of swaying palms, grass-skirted maidens, and exotic music, with enough romance for anyone.

What a false dream! While that may be true of some central Pacific islands, it certainly wasn't true for the Solomons. They were a morass of stinking, disease-ridden jungles infested with huge snakes, lizards, gigantic frogs, and rats, and the Americans had to fight their way through all this against an enemy well dug in for a fight to the death.

The islands were first visited by the sixteenth century explorer Elvera de Mendana, who expected to find the source of gold used by Solomon (after whom the islands were named) for the temple in Jerusalem. Since then, they had been occupied by Britons, Germans, and the Dutch until the Japanese took over.

The string of islands, roughly 800 miles long from Papua New Guinea to the southernmost island of San Cristobal, consists of 11,500 square miles. The largest land masses are Malaita, San Cristobal, Choiseul, New Georgia, and Guadalcanal.

Guadalcanal, the largest of the islands and the hub of this story, is ninety miles long and thirty miles wide. This gives a clear indication of the difficult task that confronted American forces when they landed in August 1942.

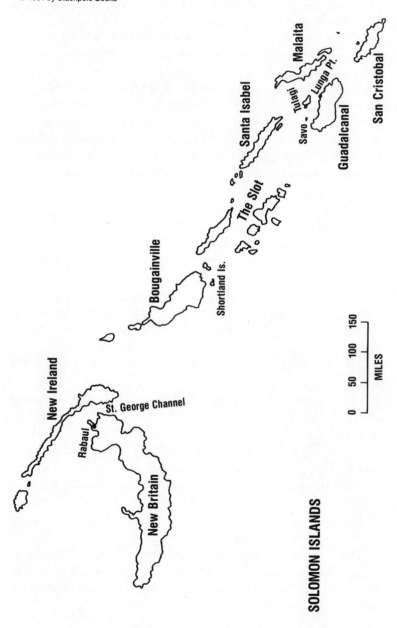

New Ireland

St. George Channel

Rabaul

New Britain

Bougainville

Shortland Is.

Santa Isabel

The Slot

Malaita

Tulagi

Lunga Pt.

Savo

Guadalcanal

San Cristobal

0    50    100    150

MILES

SOLOMON ISLANDS

When I first sailed into Guadalcanal Sound (later dubbed Iron Bottom Sound for the many sunken ships there), I marveled over its incredibly blue waters and the deep green vegetation of its islands that are so characteristic of that region of the Pacific. Even now it's difficult to comprehend that all that calm and beauty would be torn asunder by a series of savage air and naval battles.

Ahead we spotted the huge mass of Guadalcanal, with its hulking 8,000-foot mountain. To our port lay Malaita, a cucumber-shaped island with heavy, green jungles; to starboard was the southern tip of Santa Isabel Island, which snaked away to the northwest.

As we rounded the northwest tip of the Florida Islands, we spotted Savo Island, a dead volcano three miles wide by four miles long. It gave the impression of a sullen sentinel plunked squarely in the center of the sound, guarding Guadalcanal and the islands around it.

Savo certainly stirred our imaginations. Some of my buddies likened it to a humpback whale coming to the surface; others thought it to be the fin of some prehistoric monster breaking the water. One shipmate from the South said it resembled a "razorback hog wallowing in mud." To me, it looked like one of those purple snow cones one gets at a circus or carnival. At any rate, few realized that around this small island, Vice Adm. Gunichi Mikawa would soon come booming in with his cruisers and raise havoc with everything in sight.

As we passed Savo, we glimpsed the body of water that flows between it and Guadalcanal, a distance of about fourteen miles. This was the southern end of that highway of water called "the Slot" that runs all the way to New Guinea. The Slot is roughly 300 miles long and sixty miles at its widest point. This deep water highway was where we clashed with the Tokyo Express, many times at point-blank range.

Guadalcanal itself, shaped like an Idaho potato, was a fascinating place to visit, though the humidity was oppressive and we knew that enemy soldiers lurked inland. The tropical ambience was intensified by groves of palm trees, carpets of sharp kunai grass, plenty of rivers, and white, sandy beaches. In fact, the Solomons still have abundant growths of hibiscus plants and more than 230 species of orchids—a tropical plant lover's paradise.

The area from Lunga Point inland was characterized by mangrove swamps and more palms. Farther inland, some of the trees grew to a height of 150 feet. But the beauty was offset by the fetid swamps. They teemed with every species of unpleasant wildlife, like snakes, lizards, and huge mosquitoes. Towering over it all was the Kavo Range of seventeen peaks, the largest being 8,000-foot Mount Popomanasio. At times, its summit was shrouded in mist.

If nothing else, the weather was ideal—if one liked tropical climes. The daytime temperature rarely exceeded eighty-eight degrees and night temperatures were rarely below seventy. November through April was the wet season, but heavy squalls popped up anytime, especially at night. The air was always saturated with odors—at times, a stink from the swamps, at others, the sweetness of tropical flowers.[5]

So, the Solomon Islands, while not exactly a tropical paradise, are not as insufferable as many think. But, as one of my buddies remarked after looking around Guadalcanal, "I sure don't think we'll find Dorothy Lamour around here anywheres."

The Japanese saw the strategic value of Guadalcanal and its adjacent islands long before the Americans did. They had planned to occupy various islands along the Slot and seize Guadalcanal and Tulagi, then build an airfield on the former and a seaplane base on the latter.

So it was on May 3, 1942, when the sun came up and splashed the blue waters of Sealark Channel to reveal a force of Japanese transports, along with a seaplane tender and screening warships, off Tulagi. Resistance was quickly overcome by 2,000 Imperial marines. Early on July 1, airfield construction gangs crossed the sound to Lunga Point on Guadalcanal to start work.

The Japanese now had a foothold in the southern Solomons. They cast greedy eyes toward Espiritu Santo and New Caledonia to the south and, by occupying them, planned to isolate Australia from the Allies. Admiral Yamamoto moved major units of his Combined

Fleet to Truk, more than 1,000 miles to the north, and Imperial forces were beefed up at five airfields on Rabaul. Unknown to the Japanese, covetous eyes in the Pentagon were also looking at maps of the Solomons. The U.S. brass was hotly debating the merits of seizing them for an eventual climb to Tokyo. The stage was being set for the long, bitter, and bloody struggle for the Solomons.

## NOTES

1. Thaddeus Tuleja, *Climax at Midway* (New York: Berkeley Publishing Corp., 1961), p. 23.

2. Gordon Prange, *Miracle at Midway* (New York: McGraw-Hill, 1982). Perhaps the most authoritative book on the Midway battle.

3. Mitsuo Fuchida and Masatake Okumiya, "The Battle of Midway," in David C. Evans, ed., *The Japanese Navy in World War II* (Annapolis: Naval Institute Press, 1986). This book is a collection of articles by former Imperial Navy officers and offers penetrating insight into selected Pacific campaigns, including an interesting account of I-168's movements before the attack on the *Yorktown*.

4. Mitsuo Fuchida and Masatake Okumiya, *Midway: The Battle That Doomed Japan* (New York: Ballantine Books, 1955). Although I disagree with the subtitle, it is an excellent account and gives the Japanese view of the battle.

5. Robert C. Muehrcke, ed., *Orchids in the Mud* (Chicago: 132nd Infantry Regiment of World War II Association, 1985). This book, privately printed, is an account of that division's fighting and the conditions under which it took place. The book contains a unit roster; Dr. Muehrcke was a second lieutenant.

# 2
# American Resolve

In July, Adm. Ernest King, chief of naval operations, had a decision to make. With intelligence reports in hand, he urged a plan upon the Joint Chiefs of Staff for a countermove against the Japanese on Tulagi and Guadalcanal. The tall, white-haired, precise admiral knew in a flash that the occupations presaged further enemy thrusts south to New Caledonia, Samoa, and even Australia.

His plan called for an invasion of Tulagi and Guadalcanal as a first step of a "climb" up the Solomon chain to Rabaul. He argued vigorously for the plan despite the army's policy of defeating Germany first and the Rising Sun later. Many believed that the JCS were adamant that U.S. Pacific forces fight a holding action until the war in Europe looked more promising.

King asserted that Japanese air bases on these islands would seriously threaten our tenuous supply lines to Australia. He won his argument. After debating several plans, the JCS ordered up Operation Watchtower, in which American forces would seize Tulagi and Guadalcanal, removing a serious threat.

Admiral Nimitz at Pearl Harbor was ordered to expedite the plan. He grimly referred to it as Operation Shoestring, but when he snapped into action, things began to happen. Commanders were named: Vice Adm. Robert L. Ghormley was in overall charge; Admiral Fletcher of Midway fame was commander of the expeditionary force, along with the carriers *Enterprise, Saratoga,* and *Wasp*; Rear Adm. Richmond Kelly Turner was appointed commander of South Pacific amphibious forces, with four cruisers, two Australian cruisers, and nineteen transports loaded with 19,000 marines; and the flamboyant Rear Adm. Victor Charles Crutchley of the Royal Australian Navy was in charge of screening forces.

The First Marine Division was chosen to take the islands. This tough group, part of which had fought the Japanese on Wake Island, was to be commanded by Maj. Gen. Alexander Vandegrift. This was the only trained contingent available for amphibious operations.

In late July, the ships and men assembled off Koro Island in the Fijis, which approximated Guadalcanal, in order to practice landings. The first were a complete bust and the effectiveness of the invasion forces was doubted. Nevertheless, cool heads prevailed and Watchtower was ordered to proceed without delay.

At 4:00 A.M. August 7, the seventy-five-ship task force slipped through Cape Esperance and into the sound. At sea, the carrier support group protected the move. The landings succeeded at Lunga Point. Richard Tregaskis, who was on board a transport, related in his *Guadalcanal Diary* that the ship's officers were incredulous. They thought the Japanese were dumb or had some kind of trick.[1] Tulagi took longer to secure because the Imperial marines put up quite a fight. But resistance was overcome and by August 9 the southern tip of the Solomons was in American hands.

So far so good, but the ease with which the marines took the island would soon be shattered. The Japanese reaction came swiftly. A flight of Betty bombers from Rabaul stormed into the sound and crippled the destroyer *Jarvis* and the transport *George F. Elliott* before being driven off. We were always fascinated by the skill and daring of the Betty pilots in these attacks. The twin-engined bombers, which resembled our B-25s, would skim over the surface between ships, sometimes as low as fifteen feet, then lift their noses and soar over a luckless ship to "lay an egg" on it. It was difficult to get one of them because few antiaircraft guns could be depressed and friendly ships might be hit.

It was frustrating for our gunners to say the least, but we had backhanded admiration for the pilots of those Mitsubishi planes.

It is curious that the Japanese high command was caught so flat-footed by the American invasion of Guadalcanal. Somewhere, somehow, their intelligence had failed. Only light forces were on the islands and the mainstay of the Combined Fleet was riding safely in home waters. A token number of cruisers and destroyers was at Rabaul, a far cry from the massive buildup a few months earlier.

Two explanations are possible: the Japanese assumed that the Americans, having lost two fleet carriers during Coral Sea and Midway, weren't inclined or able to strike into the heart of the Imperial stronghold in the Solomons. In fact, Yamamoto felt that the Americans couldn't launch any offensive until mid-1943. It appeared that "victory fever" still afflicted the warlords.

The other possibility is that the Imperial Army brass was so preoccupied with its proposed invasion of New Guinea and the drive toward Port Moresby that it gave little thought to the Guadalcanal operation and left the show up to the navy.

How startled the Japanese must have been at American resolve!

The Americans did have a serious obstacle: Fletcher had to withdraw his carriers after dark because his pilots were not trained in night fighting. That left the Imperial ships and planes free to roam the Slot at night, setting the stage for the Tokyo Express runs. The reluctance to keep U.S. carrier forces in the area at all times was to weigh heavily in the weeks and months to come.

Marine commanders were incensed, but Admiral Turner, a crusty officer of the King mold and a former director of the War Plans Division of the Navy Department, agreed with Fletcher.

Who could blame Fletcher? He had lost two carriers and knew, more than many, the capabilities of Japanese airmen. Were he to lose just one more of his flattops, American carrier strength in the Pacific would be fatally depleted. He also knew that despite Midway, the Japanese still had more carriers than he. Furthermore, Japanese land-based aircraft in the Solomons were to be reckoned with.

"Gentlemen," he had told the commanders, "I can't keep the carriers in the area for more than forty-eight hours after the landings." [2] And that, as the man said, was that!

The reader must keep in mind the Pentagon's preoccupation with the struggle in Europe and that our Pacific forces were expected to conduct a holding operation early in the war. It was a simple matter of priorities.

The U.S. command certainly was aware of the grave situation in the Pacific, but our factories were not yet up to peak production and whatever was available was thrown into the fight against Hitler. Then, too, the United States was confident that Nimitz and Gen. Douglas MacArthur would hold the Japanese at bay until greater forces were available.

As far as we navy men in the Pacific were concerned, we'd take our ships and, as long as we had ammunition, food, and fuel, we'd do the best we could to "kick the khaki butt of old Tojo." I'm also convinced that, for some reason, we grossly underestimated Japanese military strength. For example, we began to think Yamamoto was running around the Pacific with some "super armada" because carrier-borne Zeros, Kates, and Vals would pop up all over the place. We couldn't figure out what carrier they were coming from. We later learned that these planes came from island bases, "unsinkable aircraft carriers" established by the enemy long before hostilities broke out.

One must remember that we didn't have satellites whizzing through space in those days, pointing lenses at every nook and inlet on the globe. If we had, we would have spotted this "super armada" for what it was. By the same token, the Japanese would have spotted our forces preparing for and converging on Guadalcanal.

Intelligence gathering in the 1940s, depending more on human beings, was less advanced and both sides coped with what sources they had. Electronic eavesdropping in those days simply involved listening to enemy radio communications and the breaking of codes. It was a long and tough job. As the sign in an old Western saloon said, "Don't shoot the piano player. He's doing the best he can." In 1942, the two piano players in the Solomons were doing the best they could.

## NOTES

1. Richard Tregaskis, *Guadalcanal Diary* (New York: Random House, 1943). By far the most famous and popularly read book on the campaign. For its graphic description of soldier life and the battles fought on Guadalcanal, it is highly recommended.

2. E. B. Potter, *Nimitz* (Annapolis: Naval Institute Press, 1976); E. B. Potter, *Bull Halsey* (Annapolis: Naval Institute Press, 1985).

# 3
# Who's on First on Guadalcanal?

Yamamoto had been greatly distressed over the defeat at Midway in June and had ordered a cloak of secrecy over the return of his fleet to Japan. Wounded sailors and airmen were brought ashore at heavily guarded ports and the Japanese people didn't learn of the defeat until after the war.

Yet there was much to be done. The Imperial Army had planned another attempt at Port Moresby, only this time by land, over the Owen Stanley Mountains of New Guinea. A fortress with an air and naval base had been established at Rabaul on New Britain. It had been a good decision. Rabaul, on the northern tip of the island overlooking Simpson Harbor on Blanche Bay, had a harbor ten miles across. The natural fleet anchorage was wide and deep and protected by mountains on three sides. It was the "head of the table" for the Solomons.

A glance at a map shows the strategic value of Rabaul. It commands all sea approaches to the north and looks down the Solomons clear to Guadalcanal. In May, Imperial forces had moved down the Slot and occupied Tulagi. Guadalcanal was to be next in June, with an airfield to be built there. Yamamoto formed a new fleet for the occasion, the Eighth, known operationally as the Outer South Seas Force, based at Rabaul. He picked Vice Adm. Gunichi Mikawa to command it.

It was another good choice. Mikawa, a gentle, soft-spoken man, was a brilliant tactician and a warrior in the true samurai tradition. He wasn't afraid of taking chances, either, as the fighting would show.

After a series of conferences in Tokyo and at Truk, Mikawa assembled his new force. It included the fine new heavy cruisers *Chokai* (his flagship), *Aoba, Kinusaga, Kako,* and *Furutaka*; the light cruisers *Tenryu* and *Yubari*; and four destroyers. These ships and major units of the Combined Fleet shrank the harbor at Truk.

This was not surprising. Truk, 2,000 miles from Japan, was the Empire's Pearl Harbor. It is an atoll of forty-eight islands plopped in the center of a coral reef, forty miles across and forty-five miles long. It had an anchorage of 8,823 square miles! Small wonder the entire Combined Fleet could anchor in it.

On July 26, Mikawa weighed anchor and his *Chokai* led the new Eighth Fleet out of Truk for Rabaul. The trip was to make history, since the future of the Pacific war was decided in the coming drama. The American landings on Guadalcanal were the curtain raiser.

Mikawa reached Rabaul on a sun-filled day and dropped anchor in spacious Simpson Harbor. He immediately ordered out his launch and went ashore. He and his staff were set up in a ramshackle building belonging to the Second Air Group. He called a conference to plan the coming Port Moresby operations.

The admiral, his sharp mind ready for all the facts and figures, asked, "What is the status of the New Guinea operations?"

A 17th Army commander replied, "Our troops have started up the Owen Stanley Mountains and have advanced as far as Kokoda. Your fleet must provide more troops and supplies if we are to succeed in crossing the mountains and start our assault on Port Moresby."

Another officer said, "There's increasing evidence of enemy forces around Guadalcanal. Our garrison on Tulagi reported enemy planes coming over almost daily."

Mikawa shrugged. "Merely a diversion," he said. "Fourth Fleet headquarters assures me the United States is incapable of launching large-scale counterattacks."

Then, in a surprisingly complacent move, he sent the heavy cruisers north to the Kavieng anchorage on New Ireland. He figured that he had every contingency covered. On August 7, his complacency collapsed when an aide rushed in with an urgent dispatch: "0430. Tulagi being heavily bombarded from air and sea. Enemy carrier force sighted." It became apparent that American forces backed by battleships, carriers, cruisers, destroyers, and transports had landed on Guadalcanal.

Not a procrastinator, Mikawa planned to strike back and strike hard. He sent for the cruiser division at Kavieng and ordered all aircraft to attack the Guadalcanal landing site. His plan was to take the cruisers down the Slot at night, shoot up the transports, and sink any American warships in the area. It was to be a swift and decisive blow, hopefully catching the Americans off guard. He was confident his splendid ships and crews would do the job.

And why not? His cruisers were the best in the world. His *Chokai*, for example, had impressive credentials: it displaced 11,000 tons and had ten eight-inch guns and four seven-inchers. As with most Japanese cruisers, unlike their American counterparts, she carried eight twenty-four-inch tubes firing deadly Long Lance torpedoes.[1] Small wonder Mikawa was so confident, even though enemy carriers were reported in the area. His effort was to be in the great tradition of the Imperial Navy.

The ships left Simpson Harbor and rendezvoused in St. George Channel at 7:00 P.M. August 7. Mikawa cast a critical eye over his task force, pronounced it ready, then ordered the column to barrel down the Slot toward Guadalcanal.

It is one of the ironies of this battle that Mikawa's force was never properly detected and reported during its daylight run the next day. At one point it was spotted by a patrol plane whose pilot thought that two of the cruisers were seaplane tenders. The report was bungled and didn't reach Admiral Turner for hours. Even then he dismissed it, figuring the "tenders" were headed elsewhere to set up a base. Thus Mikawa's force continued down the Slot.

Another irony was the withdrawal of Admiral Fletcher's carriers for refueling, leaving the transports at Tulagi and Lunga Point on Guadalcanal without air cover. The vessels now protecting the transports were divided into three groups: the Northern Force consisted of the heavy cruisers *Vincennes*, *Astoria*, and *Quincy* and two screening destroyers; the Southern Force was composed of the Australian heavy cruisers *Australia* and *Canberra*, the U.S. heavy cruiser *Chicago*, and two destroyers, one of which was the *Patterson*; and the transport area was patrolled by two light cruisers and a destroyer. As a further safeguard, the destroyers *Blue* and *Ralph Talbot* took up patrol on the northwest approaches to the sound.

Toward this seemingly impenetrable curtain Mikawa boldly steamed. He had formed a column, about 1,000 yards separating each ship, in the following order: the *Chokai*, followed by the *Aoba*, *Kako*, *Kinusaga*, *Furutaka*, *Tenryu*, *Yubari*, and a destroyer, the *Yunagi*, as "Tail-End Charlie." This task force had about seventy guns.

Mikawa knew what he was up against. Earlier, his cruiser floatplanes had given him a clear picture of ship dispositions in the sound (another blunder by the Americans: those planes were never fired upon). He huddled over charts with Toshikazu Ohmae, captain of military affairs of the Bureau of the Naval Ministry, who had come along on the mission.[2]

"Reports indicate enemy carriers 100 miles to the south of Guadalcanal," the admiral said. "There's no fear of air attack until morning. It would appear that all the American invasion strength is in the sound. Therefore, we'll press on with the attack."

Ohmae glanced back at the *Chokai*'s wake; it was sparkling in a phenomenon caused by the luminescence of the microorganism noctiluca, indigenous to South Pacific waters. He hoped the enemy wouldn't spot the wake by air.

"Ship approaching, thirty degrees starboard!" shouted a lookout. It was an enemy destroyer, the *Blue*! All guns were trained out, ready to blast her, but she made a ninety-degree turn and continued steaming idly southward, oblivious to the Japanese column. All hands relaxed. It was a close call and the last thing Mikawa wanted was an early engagement that would alert enemy forces ahead.

Then: "Ship sighted, twenty degrees to port!" All hands tensed again; it was the *Ralph Talbot*. But the vessel was stern on and was steaming away to the north. Incredible! Two American pickets completely blind to the Japanese juggernaut. The column entered the sound at 1:36 A.M., still undetected. Mikawa was amazed. He turned to the *Chokai*'s skipper, Mikio Hyakawa, and said, "The Americans must be asleep."

Not all were asleep in the sound, however. The *Patterson*, was patrolling with the Southern Force, guarding the transports at Beach Red on Guadalcanal. Everyone had been expecting an attack that night because of reports of heavy Japanese ship movements at Rabaul, but no one knew from which direction it would come. Most concluded it would come from the north, which offered the best approach with possible reinforcements from Truk.

Our force, now minus the cruiser *Australia*, which had been dispatched to the transport area for a commanders' conference, steamed along at twelve knots in a box formation paralleling the Guadalcanal beachhead. The *Canberra* headed the column with the *Chicago* astern. The *Bagley*, our sister ship from Destroyer Squadron

(Desron) 4, was to port of the *Canberra*, the *Patterson* off to port, both at 1,500 yards. It was black as pitch, hot and oppressive, with occasional rain squalls jogging through the area and flickers of lightning playing in the clouds. It was one of those nights spawned in hell for trouble that was soon in coming.

Suddenly, one of the *Pat*'s lookouts spotted dark shapes moving forward off the southern tip of Savo. He called it in and the skipper, Comdr. Frank Walker, sprang into action. He called for general quarters, rang up twenty knots, and called for a hard left rudder to parallel the oncoming ships. He ordered a TBS transmission to the fleet: "Warning! Warning! Strange ships entering harbor!" Then he called for a torpedo run standby.

The *Pat* swung around to allow the starboard banks of torpedo tubes to fire. Meanwhile, the five-inch-gun crews threw up star shells, followed by armor-piercing rounds. Then, from out of nowhere flares appeared, lighting up the transport area and silhouetting us. They had come from Mikawa's floatplanes. A Japanese cruiser snapped on two searchlights and the *Pat* was on center stage. This was followed by an orange-white flash that sent an incandescent streak skyward.

It's a strange and frightening thing to have one's ship lit up by enemy searchlights. Everything is splashed white, creating a bas-relief of surroundings, including chalk-white faces of your shipmates—a nightmare!

That incandescent streak of an eight-inch shell came down and, with a sickening crunch, slammed into the aft gunhouse. An explosion followed, annihilating everyone within, plus the crew of the No. 3 gun above. Shrapnel raised havoc with the No. 4 gun directly aft. The score was eight killed and eleven missing. The *Patterson* was out of the fight.

Then, to everyone's horror, we saw that the *Canberra*, ripped apart by torpedoes and large-caliber shells, had veered off to starboard and was sinking. The heavily damaged *Chicago* was nowhere to be seen (we learned later that she had taken off toward Savo Island, looking for targets, but the Japanese had gone north). The captain and crew of the American cruiser didn't seem to comprehend what was going on that night until it was too late. She survived the battle and was towed away for repairs. Meanwhile, the *Bagley* also took off

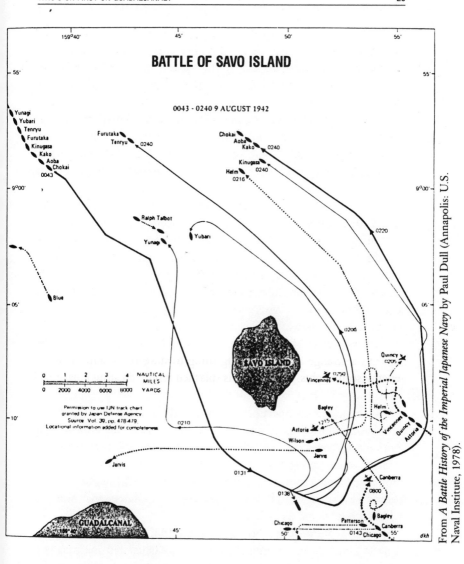

## BATTLE OF SAVO ISLAND

0043 - 0240 9 AUGUST 1942

From *A Battle History of the Imperial Japanese Navy* by Paul Dull (Annapolis: U.S. Naval Institute, 1978).

after the Japanese column but, like the *Chicago,* she found the enemy had moved too far north.

Mikawa, having mauled the Southern Force, entered a heavy rain squall as it moved north. The squall kept the Northern Force from spotting him. It would appear the weather gods had lent the wily admiral a hand. Mikawa's column had split in two as it made the northern turn (he dispatched the *Yunagi* to cover his rear flank). The starboard column was headed by the *Chokai*, the port by the *Furutaka*. The *Yubari* found itself on the *Furutaka*'s port on the run northward.

The *Chokai*, after making her northern turn, spotted the American cruisers ahead; they had just made a west turn. She snapped on her searchlights and let loose with salvo after salvo. The *Astoria* was hit amidships and burst into flames from stem to stern. The American cruisers were caught in a pincer movement!

Methodically, the Japanese pressed their surprise attack and flung round after round at the surprised Americans. The *Aoba* pumped eight-inch shells into the *Quincy* ahead of the *Astoria*.[3] The same went for the *Vincennes*, whose captain wasn't yet convinced enemy ships were around. It was a duck shoot for Mikawa. Two large-caliber shells slammed into the *Vincennes'* floatplanes amidships and turned her into a funeral pyre. Both cruisers went down. The smashed *Quincy* took the plunge at 2:05 A.M.

One of the Northern Force's screening destroyers tried to close on the enemy column but did no damage. Mikawa ignored her. The other, the *Helm*, didn't get into action. She wandered around as if in a daze.

One interesting aspect of the battle with the Northern Force was told by Captain Ohmae, who was on the bridge of the *Chokai* with Admiral Mikawa. He remembers that one of the stricken American cruisers, ablaze along her entire length, closed on the *Chokai* as if to ram. The flaming ship got one eight-inch shell into the flagship's chart room. This dying vessel was the *Astoria*, and Ohmae and Admiral Mikawa later noted its crew's bravery.[4]

After shattering the Northern Force, Mikawa's ships were in disarray. He regrouped and for a time considered returning to the area to bombard the helpless transports. However, worried over possibly being caught by American carrier planes at daylight, he decided to head back to Rabaul at high speed. It was now 2:10 A.M.

Some of Mikawa's officers complained bitterly over this decision. They wanted to finish off the transports now that they were unprotected. But the admiral was firm; he held to the policy that enemy warships were the prime targets.

Besides, the Imperial Army had informed Fourth Fleet headquarters that it would take care of the American landing forces on Guadalcanal in short order. Why bother to sink transports? Then there were the elusive American carriers. Mikawa knew from Midway what carrier planes can do to a surface force. He didn't want to sacrifice his ships in daylight, especially after such a glorious victory. (Of course, Mikawa had no way of knowing that Fletcher's flattops had retired far southward for the night. Another irony!)

Mikawa listened to his junior officers patiently, but held his ground. At 2:10 A.M., he barked, "All forces withdraw! Force in line ahead, course 320 degrees, speed thirty knots!"

One more hand was to be played in this macabre poker game. On the northwest side of Savo he encountered the picket destroyer *Ralph Talbot*, whose captain and crew were still puzzled over the action on the other side of Savo. Mikawa dispatched the *Yubari* to finish off the intruder. She was joined by the *Furutaka* and *Tenryu*, and the three cruisers pummeled the unfortunate destroyer.[5] But the *Ralph Talbot* didn't sink; she reeled off toward Savo under the protection of a rain squall. After all the carnage, three cruisers failed to sink one American destroyer!

Later that morning, as Mikawa approached Rabaul, he dispatched the *Kako* to the Kavieng anchorage.

En route, she was spotted by the American sub *S-44*, which fired four fish into her. The *Kako* sank at 8:10 A.M. with seventy-one killed and fifteen wounded. We had taken partial revenge for Savo.[6]

In retrospect, the battle of Savo Island had mixed results for both sides. The Japanese had sunk four cruisers and a destroyer (the *Jarvis*, damaged in an earlier air attack, was sunk by enemy planes the next day as she limped away from the Solomons), but they didn't destroy the transports. For the Americans, those transports and their precious cargoes were saved, but their surface force was greatly diminished. The carriers, which could have caught Mikawa in daylight, were too far away. There was enough blame to go around and two Americans paid a high price for the disaster: the skipper of the *Vincennes* was a broken man and the captain of the *Chicago* committed suicide. From official inquiries came important lessons for the U.S. Navy. There had been a deficiency of communications, faulty damage control, a sad lack of battle readiness among the crews and poor firefighting techniques. Communications were improved by better radio equipment, a new damage-control program was drilled into crews, and battle readiness was improved with a new watch-rotation program. The navy also adopted a new nozzle system in which fires are deprived of oxygen by a thick "fog," much like today's fire extinguishers. In addition, excess paint was removed because burning layers proved deadly at Savo, and wardrooms were cleared of all upholstery, linoleum, and wood. Such materials had helped incinerate some of the cruisers at Savo. But the most important lesson for the Americans was to never again be caught flat-footed, confused, and without adequate air cover. It took a while, but the U.S. Navy learned from its mistakes while the Japanese didn't, as we shall see. In time, the Americans replaced their losses; the Japanese couldn't.

In a way, Mikawa's force in the battle of Savo Island could be called the granddaddy of the Tokyo Express. The Japanese had quickly and efficiently learned to run down the Slot at night with impudence, dropping off supplies and men and boldly tangling with American ships. They used this technique with new fervor in the months to come. Admiral Mikawa's stunning victory was but a prelude to the fighting to occur in the bloody contest for the Solomons.

## NOTES

1. Anthony J. Watts and Brian G. Gordon, *The Imperial Japanese Navy* (New York: Doubleday & Co. Inc., 1971). This work, twenty years in the making, is the basic source for Japanese ship information.

2. Toshikazu Ohmae, "The Battle of Savo Island," in Evans; Richard F. Newcomb, *Savo* (New York: Bantam Books, 1961). Evans offers an eyewitness account of the battle; Newcomb gives the American perspective.

3. *Aoba* Action Report in *Tabular Records and Action Reports of Japanese Battleships and Cruisers* (TJ-1) (Washington, D.C.: Operational Archives

Branch, U.S. Navy Historical Center), Microfilm. The *Aoba*'s Action Report records one enemy heavy cruiser sunk by her torpedoes and one by gunfire, with two more cruisers damaged by gunfire.

4. Ohmae, p. 226.

5. *Tenryu* Action Report in *Action Records and Action Reports of Japanese Battleships and Cruisers.*

6. *Aoba* Action Report in *Tabular Records and Action Reports of Japanese Battleships and Cruisers.* Mentions the sight of the *Kako*'s sinking and includes a puzzling entry that reads, "Carried out embarrassing depth charge barrage." The *Aoba* later picked up the *Kako*'s survivors.

4

# Coupling Up the Tokyo Express

In late 1942, more than 19,000 American marines were fighting their way across Guadalcanal against a few detachments of Japanese troops. Imperial headquarters had underestimated American strength in the Solomons and, because of the "invincibility factor," Japan had committed only token troop strength there, concentrating on the New Guinea operation and the proposed push overland to Port Moresby, its top priority.

Remember that Japan's victories after Pearl Harbor had spread its influence over a wide area, reaching from Tokyo to Southeast Asia and from Indonesia to Melanesia and Micronesia. It was not surprising that Imperial headquarters cast a baleful glance at what was happening on "Gadarukanaru," its name for Guadalcanal.

Before Pearl Harbor, Yamamoto had told the war ministers that, with the Combined Fleet, he could give the Americans a run for their money for eighteen months. After that, when American industrial capacity had reached its peak, Japan was sure to be overwhelmed. But he hoped that after the American fleet was destroyed and the Greater East Asia Co-Prosperity Sphere had been consolidated, the Americans would sue for peace. He believed that he could lure the U.S. Navy into that decisive naval defeat, but if the fleet action did not come quickly, Japan instead would be crushed. The Imperial war councils ignored his warnings and called for the Pearl Harbor strike. He protested but the councils were adamant.[1]

Yamamoto was a good sailor and fanatically loyal to the emperor, so he swallowed his misgivings and did what was expected of him. It is ironic that Pearl Harbor was a smashing victory and that the Midway plan, about which Yamamoto was enthusiastic, was a defeat. Now the Solomons had his attention and he needed to be near the action. After the battle of the Eastern Solomons on August 24, during which Japan lost a light carrier and the Imperial troops on Guadalcanal still hadn't been reinforced, he swung into action.

On August 26, flying his flag aboard the *Musashi*, the *Yamato*'s sister ship, he led the Combined Fleet into Truk to command all naval activities in person. If there was to be a fleet action, he'd be on the spot!

The high command became badly shaken when it realized that the U.S. marines on Guadalcanal were not only holding their own but were actually wiping up Japanese units. The Imperial Army decided to reinforce the island and Yamamoto ordered the destroyers and cruisers at Rabaul to help ferry the troops. Imperial destroyermen didn't want their ships used as troop transports. In fact, after the war, destroyer skipper Tameichi Hara said that the Combined Fleet and the army had blundered when they committed destroyers piecemeal in the Solomons without adequate help from aircraft and large ships. The navy couldn't afford the heavy attrition of vessels.

Nevertheless, Combined Fleet headquarters named the best destroyerman for the job: Rear Adm. Raizo Tanaka. Brilliant and bold, the solemn-faced officer graduated from the Imperial Naval Academy in 1913, attended torpedo school in 1920, became an expert, and consequently served on destroyers, chalking up an enviable record. After Pearl Harbor, Tanaka was promoted and assigned command of the Second Destroyer Squadron. He fought at the battles of Java Sea, Coral Sea, and Midway. He was a hardened, resourceful veteran.[2]

Following the formation of the Eighth Fleet in early July, aboard his flagship *Jintsu* (it was tradition to lead such squadrons with light cruisers), Tanaka led his force of ten destroyers to Rabaul. He originated the risky runs down the Slot to reinforce the garrisons on Guadalcanal—the Tokyo Express.

Tanaka wasted no time. With his fast destroyers, he ventured down the Slot at night, dropping off his cargoes of men and supplies and then scooting back to Rabaul. His ships suffered some damage but he lost none until the Americans sought to intercept them. Of course, the Americans also realized the gravity of the situation in the Solomons. Their troops had to be supplied and Japanese forces had to be dealt with. Vice Adm. R. L. Ghormley, commander of the South Pacific Force, based on Espiritu Santo, was well aware of the situation. It was frustrating to have to withdraw air cover over Guadalcanal at night. The arrival of two fast battleships, the *Washington* and *South Dakota*, from the Atlantic improved things a bit, but he knew only too well that the Japanese outnumbered him in all types of ships. Like

Yamamoto, he tended to hoard his big ships until a situation was serious enough for them to be committed.

Also, Henderson Field on Guadalcanal was only in limited use by the new "Cactus Air Force" ("Cactus" was the U.S. code name for Guadalcanal) because of a serious shortage of planes.

So for now, the U.S. situation in the Solomons was iffy, to say the least.

Meanwhile, Gen. Douglas MacArthur, who was in Australia and had recently been appointed commander in chief of the southwest Pacific, was putting the finishing touches on his plan to conquer Japan. He wanted to seize Rabaul as a stepping-stone to the Philippines (to which he had promised to return) and from there ultimately go to Tokyo. The operation, labeled Cartwheel, called for a push up the Solomons to New Britain. Like Ghormley, he was short on aircraft, ships, and men. It's easy to imagine the wrangling that went on in command headquarters in Espiritu Santo, Noumea, and Brisbane. It was the old army vs. navy rivalry. Fortunately, both sides realized that the Solomons were the key to defeating Japan and that held them together somewhat.

At Pearl Harbor, thousands of miles away, Admiral Nimitz was forming a plan by which the drive to Tokyo would be made through the central Pacific, starting with the Kwajalein atoll. It was to be an "island-hopping" operation by which some Japanese-held islands would be taken and others would be left to wither on the vine.[3] After much interservice planning, Nimitz's and MacArthur's plans were to be combined into one master strategy, but that's another story.

It's curious that a lot of us in the Pacific at this time felt a sense of foreboding. Our derisive opinions of Japanese abilities had evaporated since Savo Island, and despite our stunning victory at Midway, we knew the Japanese still had a formidable fleet while we were in a holding action with older ships and minimal carrier strength. There were rumors about those "big bastard" battleships with eighteen-inch guns. How could we possibly counter those salvos when our biggest battleships only had sixteen-inchers? Some said that their shells weighed two tons and could be hurled more than twenty-two miles.

And we still didn't know how many carriers Yamamoto had. Eight? Ten? Twelve? But we were sure that some of our commanders had an inkling. Small wonder, then, that Ghormley hesitated to commit our precious carriers to Yamamoto's wish for a decisive battle.

That's not to say that we weren't spoiling for a fight. That American resolve, rekindled at Pearl Harbor, was still there. There were plenty of times when, during gunnery practice, we fantasized that our projectiles were slamming into enemy ships. It was a hope that kept us going during those unsettled months, though we now knew that the enemy had fast, well-armed ships with crews proficient in night fighting.

It wasn't easy to look out over inky waters and know your enemy could see better than you, in spite of our vaunted radar! Regardless of what many think, that equipment wasn't as efficient as we would have liked, except for radar-controlled gunfire. More on that later.

Still, we were supremely confident in our fighting abilities. Since when did Americans run away from a fight, especially with a big bully? Once we were steaming toward a battle area when a buddy and I had a conversation—over coffee, of course—about the situation.

"Do you think the Japs will come out and fight?" I asked.

"Bet on it," my friend the gunner's mate replied. "But if they do, we'll kick their asses clear to Tokyo."

"But suppose they bring up those big bastards?"

"Ha!" he replied. "In that case, we'd better learn to sidestep real fast!"

Such was our confidence, even against big odds. I guess that, in those disquieting days in the Pacific, it was a case of two wary opponents, each respecting the other's capabilities, circling and sparring, hoping to get in that decisive blow.

Such matters didn't concern Admiral Tanaka at Rabaul. He had a job to do and he would do it. He had studied the situation and decided that the landings in the Philippines and Celebes, among others, had shown just how difficult such operations could be. They entailed close coordination between landing forces and covering warships. Landings must achieve surprise and be preceded by a heavy bombardment.

He concluded that he could do neither at Guadalcanal and he knew he might suffer heavy losses. But he would do his best. Running down the Slot, he'd be exposed to enemy aircraft and submarines, and at the landing site he might be challenged by enemy naval units. Thus, he had to ferry and unload troops ashore as well as prepare for possible surface action. He also was concerned that he wouldn't be able to rehearse or even properly study such operations. They would be by the seat of his pants.

He knew, however, that the operation was crucial and urgent, so Tanaka marshaled his ships and planned to carry the Ichi detachment (the unit that had been scheduled to land at Midway) down the Slot and drop it off on Guadalcanal. If American destroyers and cruisers came out to challenge him, so much the better. It was to be the first real run of his Tokyo Express.

The shrewd admiral had supreme confidence, too. Both sides were convinced that they had the best men and ships. For instance, at the beginning of the war, Tanaka said Japanese torpedo forces were the best combat units in the world. But he was concerned that radar-equipped American ships would cut into night combat efficiency. Had Tanaka known that U.S. radar technology was still so new that its potential was never fully realized or used efficiently in the Solomons campaign, he might have slept better.

Still, as he looked out over the sparkling harbor as his destroyers were loaded with troops and supplies, he felt he could handle the job. His lookouts, with their supreme night-sighting skills, would help counter U.S. radar. The Imperial navy had combed the fleet for men with exceptional night vision; with their new marine glasses, they could distinguish targets at more than four miles.

He had another edge: the Long Lance, developed by the Imperial Navy in 1930. The torpedo was twenty-four inches in diameter and carried a 1,200-pound warhead up to four miles at almost fifty knots. His crews had been trained to perfection and he was sure the Americans had nothing to match them. Tanaka ordered out his launch and prepared to board the *Jintsu*. With his flag flying proudly on her yardarm, he was ready to lead the Tokyo Express.[4]

Tanaka referred to his ships as "splendid," and splendid they were. But we thought ours were pretty good, too. Since "a fighting man is no better than his weapons," we'll examine the tools that both sides used. Because of its greater forces and commitments, we'll look first at the Japanese Navy.

## NOTES

1. John Dean, *Yamamoto* (New York: Viking Press, 1965), pp. 16–19. An excellent account of Yamamoto's American stay is recorded here. Yamamoto was one of the few—and perhaps the only—Japanese naval officers to get a glimpse of American industrial potential. He became convinced that Japan could never hope to win a prolonged war with the United States.

2. Raizo Tanaka, "The Struggle for Guadalcanal," in Evans. Perhaps the most authoritative account of Tanaka's actions in the Solomons.

3. Potter, *Nimitz*, p. 210. For a detailed account of Nimitz's plan after Guadalcanal was secured in 1943, see chapter 6 of this fine book.

4. Tanaka.

5

# The Imperial Navy

In the months before Pearl Harbor, I often visited the Honolulu Public Library. It was always an enjoyable and therapeutic respite from life aboard ship. Though it amused my shipmates, I spent many happy hours reading or listening to the library's record collection. Since our potential enemy was Japan, I obtained a copy of *Jane's Fighting Ships*, that stalwart annual that still covers the world's navies. Unfortunately, there was little information on Japan because of tight security by the Imperial General Staff. It dished out information that it wanted the world to see because Japan had abrogated the Washington and London naval treaties and its ship construction was under wraps.

I viewed photos of four Japanese carriers: the *Kaga*, the *Akagi*, the *Hiryu*, and the *Soryu*. I wasn't impressed by their appearances. Unlike our streamlined and clean-looking ships, these were downright ugly. The *Kaga*, for example, was shown in a vague, heavily censored photo with biplanes on the decks and a long funnel that ran her entire port side, flaring out and emitting clouds of black smoke. What a weird ship! The battleships were equally strange. The *Fuso*, for instance, looked bulky and top-heavy, with section after section built upon her superstructure to the point that it looked as if she would capsize in the first storm that came along. What kind of vessel was this? The destroyers looked as they should—long, sleek, and heavily armed. But *Jane's* could only guess their displacement and armament because of the tight censorship.

Back aboard ship, I showed the book to a gunner's mate buddy of mine. He glanced at the *Fuso* and remarked, "It would be easy to lob a shell into that woodpile!" Studying the photos, I was left with an eerie feeling about the uncomely vessels. They struck me as being cardboard cutouts on rafts. Other shipmates, especially the torpedomen, licked their lips and said, "We'll have to fight *those*? Good God, we'll sink the whole lot of 'em in a week!" Such was the smug attitude we had toward the Japanese Navy in those early days.

Were we in for a surprise! We learned that those ships were not made of cardboard, but of steel; those biplanes had been replaced with modern Vals, Judys, and Zekes; and at Guadalcanal those "top-heavy" battlewagons flung fourteen-inch shells with such accuracy that it cost us many of our modern and good-looking ships. We had to learn the hard way that Japan had the third-largest navy in the world and it knew how to use it.

How did Japan end up with the third-largest navy? In 1922, the leading naval powers met in Washington for a disarmament conference. The race for naval parity was out of hand and there was fear of another world war. Japan figured highly in this because it had launched a construction program that threatened to put it on a par with Britain and the United States.

The reluctant conferees were the United States, Great Britain, France, Italy, the Netherlands, Portugal, Belgium, China, and Japan.

U.S. Secretary of State Charles Evans Hughes pointed out that the time had come and the conference had been called, not for a general resolution or mutual advice, but for action on the limits of naval disarmament. He made it clear that they were dealing with a world-threatening situation. Despite their reluctance, the delegates were deeply concerned.

After much wrangling and debating, it was decided that 1,878,073 tons of combat ships would be scrapped. Great Britain and the United States were each to have 525,000 tons; Japan was allowed 315,000 tons of capital ships.

The Japanese were disgusted, their hopes of parity with the United States and Great Britain dashed. They scrapped a battleship and started converting three more hulls into carriers.

The warlords then determined that if the number of ships were to be limited, the ships they had would be the best the world had ever seen. The word went out to plan and build new classes of cruisers with eight-inch guns and torpedo tubes. Thus the keels of the *Kako* class were laid down.

In 1930, a London conference was called because of the many treaty violations. After this meeting, the United States was limited to 464,000 tons of capital ships (fifteen ships) and Japan to 272,070 tons (nine ships). The United States was allowed eighteen cruisers and Japan twelve, none larger than 10,000 tons.[1] The Japanese went home happier this time; now they surely would have the third-largest navy in the world! As time went on, though, the Japanese soured on the limitations. In 1934, Japan withdrew from the two pacts and started a massive buildup. Plans were drawn and keels laid for the world's largest battleships, the *Yamato* and the *Musashi*, each displacing 64,000 tons and armed with eighteen-inch guns. The Imperial Navy also embarked on an ambitious program of destroyer torpedo tactics that was to pay off at Guadalcanal.

These events give a good grasp of why Japan became a mighty naval power. At the beginning of World War II, it had ten battleships, ten carriers, eighteen heavy cruisers, twenty light cruisers, one hundred eight destroyers, and more than sixty submarines. A far cry from the collection of oddball ships in that copy of *Jane's*!

Those 108 destroyers are of particular interest because they were the main force behind the Tokyo Express. The destroyer, used by practically all navies, ran from 1,500 to 2,000 tons and was armed with three to six five-inch guns, torpedoes, and depth charges. The crews ranged from 200 to 275. Affectionately referred to as "tin cans" by those who served on them, destroyers protected battleships and carriers from submarines, aircraft, and other destroyers. Later in the war, they would also serve as antiaircraft screens.

Some of those 108 destroyers with which Japan began the war had been built as far back as 1920, but most were newer. The Japanese Navy first became aware of the importance of the destroyer at the outbreak of World War I, when, as an ally of Great Britain and France, it declared war on Germany. Realizing they were woefully short of vessels to protect the fleet, Imperial officials embarked on the War Emergency Program of 1914 and began building destroyers in earnest. Most of the early ships were nothing more than torpedo boats of 300 to 600 tons. In 1915, the Imperial Navy began building ships of 1,000 tons with 4.7-inch guns and six torpedo tubes.

In 1920, Japan designed a series of larger, faster ships. This generation spawned the models that it possessed at the outbreak of war. Designers built upon predecessors, incorporating their best features. The class of 1925 featured the "swan's neck" bow that came to distinguish Imperial ships. The design allowed the ships to cleave through the water far better than vessels with the curved bow. The forecastle, flared at the sides, also improved speed. Many times during close combat we distinguished friend from foe by that bow.

The *Fubuki* class of 1928–31 was the prototype of all future destroyers. It sported twin five-inch guns in three turrets, nine twenty-four-inch torpedo tubes, and new hydraulic ammunition lifts. It was one of the Imperial Navy's finest hours.

This led to the famous *Kagero* class of 1940–41, the epitome of Japanese destroyers, designed to counter the *Fletcher*-class American destroyers. The *Kagero*s were 388 feet long, displaced 2,033 tons, had a speed of thirty-five knots, and were armed with three five-inch twin-mount turrets and eight twenty-four-inch shielded torpedo tubes. Each had a crew of 240.[2] These "greyhounds of the sea" gave the American destroyer fleet a run for its money during the Solomons campaign with their high speed and sixteen-torpedo complements. Though we didn't know it at the outbreak of the Pacific war, Japan's fleet of destroyers was considered by many to be among the finest in the world.

The Japanese also committed some cruisers to the Guadalcanal struggle. Mikawa's flagship at the battle of Savo Island was the heavy cruiser *Chokai*, accompanied by the *Kinusaga*, the *Aoba*, the *Kako*, and the *Furutaka* and the light cruisers *Tenryu* and *Yubari*. All except the *Kako*, of course, took part in subsequent battles in the Slot. The heavy cruiser *Takao* and the light cruiser *Nagara* played a part later. But perhaps the most famous cruiser was Admiral Tanaka's flagship, the *Jintsu*. She was a workhorse with her screening destroyers and participated in many campaigns after Pearl Harbor, only to be sunk in the battle of Kula Gulf in July 1943.

The *Jintsu*, one of six in the *Sendai* class, was 500 feet long, displaced 5,195 tons, and was armed with seven five-inch guns and eight torpedo tubes. Her unusual stack arrangement—four thin and one fat—was easily identifiable at night. The *Jintsu* was formidable and her use of torpedoes in the Solomons struggle amazed the Americans, as cruisers weren't supposed to have torpedo tubes!

In the first and second battles of Guadalcanal, the Tokyo Express was buttressed by the battleships *Hiei* and *Kirishima*. The United States brought up the *Washington* and the *South Dakota* and, for the first time in the Solomons, there was a duel between dreadnoughts. What a melee that was! The Japanese outclassed us in battlewagons early in the war—ten Imperial ships to the Americans' two—so it was inevitable that Yamamoto would commit the big fellows to action early on. As we shall see, the commitment was too little, too late.

Before the Washington Treaty, Japan had a few dreadnoughts limited to twelve-inch guns. Its first step into the world of big-gunned capital ships was in 1911, when it ordered the *Kongo* from the Vickers Shipyards of Britain. It wanted to study the shipbuilding methods of the world's top fighting navy. The *Kongo* boasted fourteen-inch main armament and six-inchers in her secondary. This enabled Japan to build the powerful fleet of battleships it had at the outbreak of the Pacific war. Following the *Kongo* came the *Haruna*, the *Kirishima*, and the *Hiei*, all built in Japanese shipyards and rated among the best in the world in their category, designed to defeat American sea power. It was the golden era of the Imperial Navy's "battle line" outlook. During the war, Japan put into action the superbattleships *Yamato* and *Musashi*, but carrier battle fleets had outmoded them.

The *Hiei* and the *Kirishima* were formidable vessels, displacing 26,000 tons, capable of 27.5 knots, and armed to the teeth with fourteen-inch guns. They gave our forces a gigantic headache during the fateful nights of November 1942. Their sisters *Kongo* and *Haruna* got into the act by bombarding Henderson Field with more than 900 large-caliber shells and fifty-four five-inch projectiles. The results were devastating, setting back American air power in the Solomons for a long time. In fact, the marines called this action simply the Bombardment.

Other battleships were with Combined Fleet at the battle of Santa Cruz, but since it was primarily an air conflict, they didn't take part.

Never forget Imperial planes. They were used to bomb, strafe, or torpedo our ships and to bomb the troops on Guadalcanal. Large fleets of planes were based at Rabaul, New Guinea, and elsewhere. The success of Japan's air fleets was a startling setback to the United States because we were so ignorant of its carrier- and land-based planes. In fact, Gen. Claire Chennault tried to warn Washington in 1941 about the Zero, an amazing new fighter he'd seen over China. He was ignored. In those early days, the Allies had a misguided habit of referring to this plane as the Zeke, thinking it was another class.

Japanese aircraft construction kept pace with warship building before the war. Long before Pearl Harbor, Japan's leading aircraft manufacturers—Mitsubishi, Nakajima, and Kawasaki—had been building excellent combat planes. The United States had quite a time building aircraft to counter them. The Japanese identified their planes by numbers according to the year they were built. "Type 97" would have been built in 1937, "Type 98" in 1938, and so forth. American intelligence preferred to refer to them with Christian names: Judy, Jake, Jill, and so on. After 1940, it became easier, because the Japanese used only a single digit, such as the Type 0 (Zero) of 1940.

Many of these planes appeared in the Solomons, especially the Bettys. Others included the Zero and the Kate. The Zero was perhaps the most famous Japanese fighter. It had a top speed of 336 mph and was armed with two machine guns and two cannons. Its speed and amazing maneuverability made it the nemesis of American pilots in the early days of the war. Indeed, when they met a Zero for the first time, they were perplexed at its ability to dart about like a hummingbird. It was an awesome sight to see a Zero fighter in aerial combat. It almost seemed capable of moving sideways. In some instances, when being pursued, a Zero would suddenly nose up, flip over in a wide arc, and end up behind its pursuer, leaving a startled American pilot looking at his tail! It was the last sight many U.S. pilots saw. Navy men in the Pacific had an almost astounding respect for the Zero. It had one weakness: its light armor, sacrificed for speed. It just couldn't withstand many hits. Unfortunately for us, it was some time before U.S. pilots found that out.[3]

The Kate was the Imperial Navy's ace-in-the-hole dive bomber, used so effectively at Pearl Harbor and in other major sea battles. Highly advanced for its time, the plane could carry a torpedo or three 500-pound bombs and had an engine of up to 1,115 horsepower. The Kate and Zero were common sights during the first years of the war. Based on carriers and land, they virtually seemed to be everywhere. In fact, Kates were responsible for much of the damage to our carriers.

I had my own encounter with a Kate during our initial landings in Lingayen Gulf on Luzon in the Philippines in January 1945. I was manning a 20mm gun on the flying bridge of the attack transport *Pierce* anchored near the beach. Two kamikaze planes slipped in under our radar screens and attacked the ships. One was shot down but the other headed straight for my ship, probably because the *Pierce* flew a flag officer's pennant.

The Kate came on steadily and I kept firing at him. I knew I had hit the plane, but it wouldn't be deterred. Suddenly, when it was so close that I could count the cylinders in its radial engine, the pilot veered off. As he passed, the pilot, wearing the traditional headband, waved as if to say, "Congratulations. I have spared you." He banked and flew in a wide circle between ships, came around, and crash-dived into our sister ship to starboard, killing virtually all on the bridge! It was unforgettable.

So, even during the final days of the war, we still had a healthy respect for Japanese planes with Christian names!

With such weapons, it's easy to understand why the Imperial Navy's brass was so confident. "The American Navy is not able to field enough ships and planes to counter us in the Solomons!" the admirals crowed. "Those ships and planes cannot possibly match ours." They were right and wrong. While we didn't match the Imperial Navy's quantity of ships and aircraft, we had an advantage in quality going for us. We had the finest in ship construction technology, radar search, and fire control equipment and well-trained crews with high morale.

## NOTES

1. Oscar Theodore Barck, Jr., and Nelson Manfred Blake, *Since 1900: A History of the United States in Our Time* (New York: Macmillan, 1952), chapter 18.

2. Watts and Gordon, pp. 283-85.

3. Masatake Okumiya and Horoshiki Jiro, *Zero* (New York: Ballantine Books, 1956).

# 6

# Nimitz's Second Team

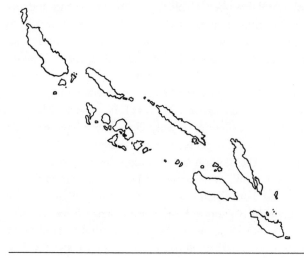

It was a typical early summer's day in sun-splashed San Diego Bay in 1941. The decks of the anchored destroyer *Patterson* were hot and had it not been for the breezes coming in from the ocean, it would have been uncomfortable. I was sitting in the shade of A turret on the forecastle, jawing with a boatswain's mate and watching raucous seagulls skim over the water, looking for food. As usual, the prospect of war was on our minds, considering the desperate situation in Europe.

"Do you think we'll go to war with Japan?" I asked.

"Possibly," the boatswain's mate said. "If we do, you can be sure this old gal and her sisters will take the brunt of it. Good old Uncle Sam's sent a lot of our tin cans to help out the Limeys in the Atlantic. So, bank on it, old buddy. We'll be plenty busy in the beginning of any clambake in the Pacific."

A few weeks later, I gazed at the mighty fleet anchored in Pearl Harbor and somehow my friend's words didn't seem so prophetic. I counted eight battleships moored at Ford Island, nine heavy cruisers anchored nearby, two carriers at the Navy Yard, and twenty to thirty destroyers moored at the East and Middle lochs. I figured that we could whip both the German and Japanese navies with one hand tied behind our back.

The events on December 7, 1941, proved me wrong and my friend right. We lost those mighty battleships; the carriers were out to sea—God knows where—and carnage was everywhere. But at least with the carriers afloat, we still had a shot at the Japanese. We also knew that the "small boys" would have to do much of the work. At the beginning of the war, the United States had seventeen battleships, thirty-seven cruisers, seven carriers, and 171 destroyers. Many of these ships were in the Atlantic, so only eight battleships, nineteen cruisers, and fifty-four destroyers were in the Pacific.

Because of the Washington and London treaties, navies converted some battleship hulls into carriers. Many of us realized that all those battleships at Ford Island had been outmoded in one fell swoop; Adm. Chuichi Nagumo's Pearl Harbor strike force did that. In fact, whether or not he knew it, the good admiral instantly relegated those revered members of all navies to second-class status. Not that it really mattered. Most of the battleships at Pearl Harbor were built between 1915 and 1921 and were essentially throwbacks to the "battle line" tactics of the Jutland era.

President Roosevelt told Congress on January 6, 1942: "The superiority of the united nations in munitions and ships must be so overwhelming that the Axis nations can never hope to catch up to it. And in order to maintain this superiority, the United States must build planes and tanks and guns and ships to the utmost limit of the national capacity."[1] For the time being, though, the forces in the Pacific had to do with what they had. It wasn't much.

Our interest is mainly with the "small boys," the Pacific destroyer fleet. These are the ships that primarily fought the Tokyo Express. Many of the Pacific destroyers at that time had been built in the 1930s. Only after the struggle began did the new *Fletcher* class trickle into the Pacific to counter the vast Japanese destroyer fleet.

The *Patterson*, like her sisters of the *Craven* class, the *Bagley*, the *Blue*, the *Ralph Talbot*, the *Mugford*, and the *Jarvis*, were joined by older ships of the *Mahan*, *Porter*, and *Farragut* classes. These vessels were stretched thin in the attempt to protect as many areas of the Pacific as possible. The nation owes them a lot.

A destroyer was considered a thing of beauty by those who sailed them. Long, sleek, and with a lethal punch, these ships could cleave the water at thirty-five to thirty-seven knots and were amazingly maneuverable. They could run rings around their bigger brethren and their heavy armament made them ideal for fighting at close quarters in the Solomons. The Japanese certainly used them well in the Tokyo Express runs—darting in and out, dropping off troops and supplies, and turning on challengers to scrap like bull terriers. While in a couple of instances the "heavies" were brought up by both sides, they couldn't maneuver in those confined waters like the "small boys" could.

A destroyer was self-contained. It had living quarters; power, cooling, and heating systems; refrigerators; water distillers; a pharmacy and sick bay; and stores for candy, soap, tobacco, and other goods. On larger ships, there usually was a library and a space for movies. We merely rigged a screen on the fantail and put a projector atop the No. 3 gunhouse. We really wished for a soda fountain, though. When we'd tie up alongside a destroyer tender, we would head straight for the soda fountain. I don't think the tender crews ever understood our craving for ice cream sodas!

The frontline destroyers of the Pacific Fleet ranged from 241 to 380 feet long, displaced 1,500 to 2,000 tons, and had a beam of thirty-four to thirty-nine feet.[2] The *Patterson* had four five-inch guns, sixteen torpedo tubes (eight on each side), and depth charges and could steam at 36.5 knots. The *Fletcher*s displaced 2,000 tons and were 370 feet long and thirty-nine feet abeam. Their five five-inch guns packed a wallop and 39,000-horsepower turbines drove them at thirty-seven to thirty-eight knots. The Japanese were particularly dismayed over the arrival of these ships. They knew the *Fletcher*s were designed to match their touted *Kagero* class.

Imagine a football field, 360 feet long and 160 feet wide. The *Patterson* could have been placed on the center of the field with 9½ feet to spare in each end zone and fifty-seven feet to spare on the sidelines. A crew of 250 had to live on this "football field" for months at a time. A destroyer operated in squadrons within divisions.

A squadron was composed of four to six ships, but the number varied in the early days. Ships often were borrowed from one squadron or another. Unlike the Japanese, who used light cruisers as squadron leaders, the U.S. Navy used a destroyer leader. Our Desdiv 4 was led by a larger ship, the *Selfridge* of the *Porter* class. She had eight five-inch guns in double turrets, twelve 20mm antiaircraft guns, and ten torpedo tubes, and could steam at thirty-seven knots. The *Selfridge* compiled a distinguished record in the Pacific war.

Other ships were involved in the battles for the Solomons. Of nineteen heavy and light cruisers in the Pacific, rarely more than three or four participated at a time during the seven battles. Typical of America's "heavies" was the *Northampton*, a member of a class of five cruisers. Although they lacked some of the credentials of their Imperial counterparts, including torpedo tubes, these cruisers were nevertheless first-rate fighting ships. The *Northampton* displaced 9,050 tons, was 582 feet long, carried nine eight-inch guns, and could steam at thirty-three knots. The *Atlanta* was one of a class of eleven light cruisers, displacing 6,000 tons. She was 541½ feet long and 53¼ feet wide and could make thirty-two knots. She was armed with sixteen five-inch guns, ten 20mm antiaircraft guns, and eight torpedo tubes. She was sunk in the first battle of Guadalcanal on November 13, 1942.

Life aboard a cruiser was a bit more comfortable, if such a term can be used to describe a warship. The quarters were larger and generally there was more than one mess hall to feed the crew of 800 to 1,000. It also had a soda fountain, large ship's stores, and a library. Cruisers were especially effective because they were among the first to have radar-directed fire control. During a scrap with the Tokyo Express, it was not unusual for the cruisers to get first hits on enemy ships. Still, they couldn't quite make the fast turns and maneuvers needed in a "gunnel-to-gunnel" fight.

Then there were the battleships. They participated in two of the seven engagements with the Tokyo Express—the first and second battles of Guadalcanal. The *Washington* and *South Dakota* had just been sent from the Atlantic because our battlewagon fleet had been destroyed at Pearl Harbor. Both these giants slugged it out with Japanese battleships in these contests.

The first fast battleships, produced in 1940, displaced 35,000 tons and were 729 feet long and 108 feet wide. They could steam at twenty-eight knots. The main armament consisted of nine sixteen-inch guns, twenty five-inch guns, sixteen antiaircraft guns, and three seaplanes. The crew totalled 2,500. The *Washington* would cover two football fields! Standing on her stern, the *Iowa* would be taller than the Pan Am building in New York!

It is difficult to describe the awe we felt from being near one of these "big boys." Their massiveness was overwhelming and their superstructures appeared to reach for the sky. And those big guns! The power of the ships lay in their radar-directed sixteen-inch guns, which could hurl 1,500-pound projectiles more than twenty miles. I've always thought it was sad that these mighty ships were outmoded by vessels with planes on their decks. In spite of their incredible armament, the battleships took their lumps in the Solomons; one was even damaged by a Japanese battleship with fourteen-inch guns. More about that later.

Meanwhile, the "small boys" did most of the tap dancing with the enemy destroyers in the Slot on those fateful nights in October and November 1942. A destroyer was a remarkable weapon in skilled hands and most of the men who commanded and sailed them were cut from rugged cloth. Its complement included a commanding officer, who could be a commander, lieutenant commander, or lieutenant. He was always called "captain" regardless of rank. Under him was the executive officer, who was in charge of the general maintenance of the ship, and the navigator. Departmental officers varied from ship to ship, but generally included engineering, damage control, gunnery, supply, torpedo, communications, and medical officers. All had enlisted men under them who ranged from seaman first and second class to chief petty officer. Like a capital ship, a destroyer was well organized and could operate independently if it had to. For example, it was not unusual for a scrappy "small boy" to take on a more powerful ship. In the battle of Samar in the Philippines on October 25, 1944, three American destroyers slugged it out with several Japanese heavies, inflicting major damage but suffering mortal hits themselves. *Johnson*, *Hoel*, and *Samuel B. Roberts* are emblazoned forever in the annals of the navy.

## NOTES

1. Hans-Adolph Jacobsen and Arthur L. Smith, Jr., *World War II Policy and Strategy: Selected Documents with Commentary* (Claremont, Calif.: Regina Books, 1979), p. 190.

2. Paul H. Silverstone, *U. S. Warships of World War II* (Annapolis: U.S. Naval Institute Press, 1989). The best source of technical information on U.S. ships.

# 7
# Tanaka's Overture

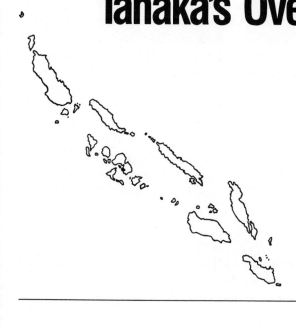

**O**n board the unlovely, four-stacked *Jintsu* in the vast Truk harbor on August 15, 1942, Adm. Raizo Tanaka studied a detailed order from the Eighth Fleet commander at Rabaul. The situation on Guadalcanal was worsening. The Americans seemed to be there to stay and were finishing the airfield begun by the Japanese. The night battle of Savo Island on August 9 had seriously hurt Allied naval forces in the area but it had not driven them from the Solomons. Something had to be done quickly.

Tanaka had been named commander of the Guadalcanal Reinforcement Force and ordered to take over Desdiv 4 and Desdiv 17 and patrol boats 1, 2, 34, and 35. He was then to proceed to the Solomons with troops, including the crack Ichiki detachment, on transports. He sat back in his chair and shook his head in disbelief. He told his aide, "This order calls for an operation to land troops on Cape Taivu on the 23rd in the face of the enemy. It is to be carried out by mixed units with no opportunity for study and rehearsal. Eighth Fleet must be in confusion."

"We still don't have a clear picture of enemy sea and air forces in the area," the aide remarked, "and we must have cover from our air forces."

Tanaka rose, went to the bulkhead, and glanced at units of the Second and Third fleets at anchor, including the huge carriers *Shokaku* and *Zuikaku* and the smaller *Ryujo* beyond. The task would be easier if these flattops were along, but he knew they wouldn't be. He sighed and turned around. "Nevertheless, orders are orders. The operation is ordained and must be carried out. We will load and depart for Guadalcanal as soon as possible, even if it takes all night."

The next morning, six destroyers loaded with the Ichiki troops headed south at twenty-two knots. Next went two gunboats (old destroyers converted into high-speed transports) escorting two army transports, the *Boston Maru* and the *Daifuku Maru*, with ammunition and supplies. Following was the fast transport *Kinryu Maru* with the Yokosuka Fifth Special Naval Landing Force, escorted by two gunboats. The *Jintsu* then rendezvoused with the flotilla and all set course for the Solomons. Along the way, Tanaka received word from Eighth Fleet headquarters that three more destroyers and a cruiser division would be added to his force. He relaxed a bit. Perhaps with these units, the task force would have a better chance.

On the eighteenth a radioman handed Tanaka a report that the advance destroyers had arrived at Cape Taivu and unloaded the 900-man Ichiki detachment with no opposition. Tanaka turned to the *Jintsu*'s captain. "So far so good," he said. "No enemy surface forces reported in the Guadalcanal vicinity. Order Desdiv 17 to return to Rabaul, leaving *Kagero, Hagikaze,* and *Yamakaze* to guard the landing area."

The next day, as the slow convoy zigzagged at 8.5 knots, Tanaka received another radio report: "*Hagikaze* hit by bombs from B-17s. Heavily damaged." He was jolted. What's this? B-17s? Where did they come from? As far as he knew, no enemy planes were operating from the Guadalcanal airfield. He concluded they must have come from Espiritu Santo. "Order *Yamakaze* to escort *Hagikaze* back to Truk for repairs!" he barked. "*Kagero* is to stay and protect the landing site."

The next morning, Tanaka learned that the *Kagero* had also been bombed, this time by carrier planes, but she wasn't seriously damaged. A reconnaissance plane reported an American carrier force 250 miles southeast of Guadalcanal. That would put carrier planes within easy striking distance of the island. Tanaka was deeply worried. Without air cover, his convoy would be a sitting duck. He thought of those big carriers back at Truk. When would Rear Adm. Aritomo Goto engage this enemy fleet? Furthermore, where were his own orders, in light of these developments?

As if in answer, he received another radio dispatch. Vice Adm. Nishizo Tsukahara, commander of the South East Area, ordered him to turn about and head north. Soon afterward, he received an order from the Eighth Fleet at Rabaul to set course for the west-southwest. Tanaka had directly contradicting orders! He walked to the bridge wing and peered at the slow-moving transports and destroyers. What to do? Obviously, he had to take some kind of independent action.

"Change course to three-twenty degrees!" he told the *Jintsu*'s skipper. "Send *Kawakaze* to relieve *Kagero.*" He watched as the 1,685-ton destroyer kicked up a wake and disappeared over the horizon at thirty knots. Then he retired to his cabin. Events would have to unfold by themselves now. His rest wasn't long. At 2:20 P.M., a radio operator handed him a message: "Twenty enemy carrier planes landed on Guadalcanal airstrip. Ichiki detachment wiped out in effort to recapture airfield."

Tanaka was saddened. The soldiers of his friend, Col. Kiyono Ichiki, without artillery support, had been cut down during an assault. Had the army underestimated American strength on Guadalcanal? When will it wake up and conduct operations intelligently there? Also, the reports of American planes on the airfield were bad news; his landing force could be jeopardized. Tanaka didn't sleep well that night.

The next morning, on the 21st, an excited radioman handed him a message from Eighth Fleet headquarters. The Second and Third fleets with their carriers would sortie into Guadalcanal waters to support his operation and engage the enemy carrier force. At last, the Combined Fleet was making a definitive move and perhaps now Yamamoto would have his decisive engagement. A major naval victory now would raise the morale of Imperial forces in the Solomons.

He turned to the south and sent the patrol boats to the Shortlands for fueling. He was heartened. His schedule called for a landing on the 23rd and, with the Combined Fleet about to draw American carrier forces away, including those planes on Guadalcanal, his chances were improved. Then came word that two enemy transports and a light cruiser had been spotted south of Guadalcanal. He ordered the destroyers *Kawakaze* and *Yunagi* to engage them.[1]

That force, a small convoy approaching Guadalcanal from the south, was entering Indispensable Strait. The destroyers *Blue*, *Henley*, and *Helm* were escorting two supply ships. The strait was black as pitch and Comdr. R. H. Smith, who was leading the force, peered out from the bridge of the *Blue*, wondering if the enemy were near. All day, reports had been coming in about Japanese ship movements in the Solomons, but he was sure his three destroyers could handle any problems.

The navigator told Smith that they were off Taivu Point and all convoy captains were told to prepare for unloading and landing. He had much-needed supplies for the troops on the island. Just then, a radio operator handed a message to the ship's captain, Comdr. H. N. Williams, who read it and handed it to Smith. Admiral Turner had ordered the *Blue* and the *Henley* to intercept an enemy flotilla headed for Lunga Point.

The destroyers broke off, leaving the *Helm* on guard, and sped toward the sound off Savo Island. When they reached Iron Bottom, the *Blue*'s radar operator reported a ship at 5,000 yards making twenty to fifty knots. (Radar gear in the early days wasn't as reliable or as precise as later equipment.) The two destroyers slowed to ten knots and began a cat-and-mouse game with the intermittent radar contacts. Curiously, both ships held their fire after the sightings, even after the target closed to 3,000 yards. Smith wasn't sure that it was not a U.S. patrol boat.

Suddenly, a lookout on one of the bridge wings shouted, "Torpedo!" Williams ordered a sharp turn, but it was too late. The stern exploded like a bomb and, her fantail in a shambles, the *Blue* began to founder. The *Henley* came over to guard her stricken sister and it soon became apparent that her steering was gone. The *Henley* passed lines over and took her in tow back to Lunga Point. Towing a stern-shattered ship is difficult—the lack of rudder control causes "fishtailing"—and it became apparent she couldn't be towed back to Espiritu Santo for repairs.

Turner decided to scuttle the *Blue* because a large enemy naval force was bearing down on Guadalcanal and she must not fall into its hands. So this star-crossed member of Desdiv 4 that had had picket duty off Savo Island on August 9 joined other ships on Iron Bottom Sound.[2] The *Blue*'s assailant turned out to be the *Kawakaze*, which quickly radioed Tanaka that she had torpedoed and sunk a destroyer. So a precious American ship was lost, with eight men dead and twenty-two wounded, because of indecision about whether to attack a fast-approaching, unidentified target. It would be a long time before this kind of reticence was corrected.

Events were coming to a head in the Solomons. Tanaka's convoy was slowly approaching from the northeast. There were reports of enemy air activity on the 24th and he fully expected an attack, but it never came. It was quiet on the bridge of the *Jintsu*, but all hands were on high alert. Suddenly, a lookout shouted, "Ships hull-down to port!" Tanaka grabbed his binoculars, fully expecting to see enemy ships bearing down on him, but he recognized the light carrier *Ryujo*, the heavy cruiser *Tone*, and two destroyers.

The admiral relaxed. He knew that the *Ryujo* group had been sent as an indirect escort to his convoy and that she was headed south so her planes could bomb the airfield on Guadalcanal.

In the meantime the *Kagero* had rejoined the convoy. Tanaka was ordered by Second Fleet headquarters to turn about until more was known about the carrier battle to the northeast. He studied the reports on the battle between the Combined Fleet and a powerful American force of "three carriers, one battleship, seven cruisers, and a number of destroyers." A last report told of "two enemy carriers set on fire," so he ordered the convoy to proceed toward Guadalcanal. The unloading would proceed on schedule. Tanaka studied the navigation charts. He was now within 150 miles of his destination and it had become daylight at 6:00 A.M. He was about to issue formation orders when a lookout shouted, "Planes overhead!"

Six American carrier planes suddenly screamed out of the sky. Two targeted the *Jintsu*, the largest of the warships. Explosions raised huge geysers around her, then a bomb landed on the forecastle directly between A and B turrets. Tanaka was flung back against a bulkhead and knocked unconscious. When he came to, unhurt, he found his beloved flagship battered, on fire and with many casualties. Luckily, no magazines were hit. Tanaka was furious with himself. The force had been caught napping. Such complacency could be fatal. He'd never allow it to happen again!

He sent the flagship back to Truk for repairs, under the escort of the destroyer *Suzukaze*, and transferred his flag to the *Kagero*. When he got on board, he learned that the *Kinryu Maru*, with 1,000 troops aboard, had been hit and was sinking. Tanaka wasted no time. He ordered the *Mutsuki* alongside the stricken transport to unload the troops, which she did. Later someone cried, "Bombers overhead!"

All eyes went skyward. B-17s had appeared and rained bombs on the transports and screening ships. Amid fire and smoke, the *Mutsuki* disappeared, followed by the *Kinryu Maru*. Luckily, most of the troops had been taken off by the destroyer *Yayoi* and two gunboats.

"This is intolerable!" Tanaka said to the skipper of the *Kagero*. "We cannot proceed to unload the remaining troops on Guadalcanal. Report to headquarters that I'm ordering all ships of this force to the Shortlands." The battered convoy headed for the anchorage with Tanaka fully expecting an end to the operation. However, along the way, he was ordered by the Eleventh Air Fleet to land the remaining 390 troops on Guadalcanal during the night of August 27. Tanaka was perplexed. He felt that it was a hasty decision, but he would carry out the new orders quickly and efficiently. His flotilla reached the Shortlands on the 27th and he immediately prepared for the re-scheduled reinforcement run.[3]

Why did Tanaka choose the smaller Shortland anchorage over that of Rabaul, with its spacious harbor and airfields? The Shortland Islands are off the southern tip of Bougainville. The largest was named after a Lieutenant Shortland of the Royal Navy after his visit there in the eighteenth century. The islands contained a natural small anchorage with two channels or passageways. They offered smaller Japanese fleet units—destroyers, light cruisers, and transports—haven from the air and sea. Most important, they cut 462 miles from the Rabaul-Guadalcanal run.

While the troops and munitions were being transferred to the destroyers *Umikaze*, *Yamakaze*, and *Isokaze*, Tanaka met with the army commander and laid out a plan for the run. The remaining 390 troops, with artillery and enough supplies for 1,300 men, would run down the Slot and unload at Cape Taivu at 9:00 P.M. August 27. The destroyers would then return to the Shortlands as quickly as possible. Tanaka would stay at the anchorage and command the operation from the *Kagero*.

The Japanese kept a wary eye on the skies, but no planes had been sighted for a couple of days. Perhaps they were involved in the carrier battle. No further word had been received on this engagement because of poor radio transmissions. Tanaka thought that poor communications could plague the Imperial Navy for the rest of the war if nothing were done.

Early in the morning on the 27th, the destroyers were ready for departure. The three vessels, bursting at the gunwales with troops and supplies, filed out of the north channel and set course for Guadalcanal. As fate would have it, the Eighth Fleet changed the landings to the 28th. Frustrated, Tanaka recalled the ships until the next day, when the run was made successfully.

Thus began the Tokyo Express runs. The Japanese and Americans were to be embroiled in a series of savage battles that neither had foreseen or wanted. During all this, a major carrier battle was raging to the northeast of the Solomons.

## NOTES

1. Tanaka; Tomeichi Hara with Fred Saito and Roger Pineau, *Japanese Destroyer Captain* (New York: Ballantine Books, 1961). Many of these conversations aren't recorded verbatim anywhere but have been carefully reconstructed from available information.

2. Theodore Roscoe, *U.S. Destroyer Operations in World War II* (Annapolis: U.S. Naval Institute Press, 1953). Contains a graphic description of the *Blue*'s destruction.

3. Tanaka, pp. 169–70.

8

# The Battle of the Eastern Solomons

The vast Truk lagoon was calm and the air muggy on August 21, 1942, as the flagship *Yamato* sat at anchor. Around her were two fleet carriers, one light carrier, three battleships, thirteen cruisers, thirty destroyers, and swarms of auxiliary vessels. As usual, the lagoon appeared shrunken by an Imperial armada. In his spacious cabin, Admiral Yamamoto sat at a table covered with maps, charts, documents, and empty teacups. Watching their commander in chief closely were four flag officers: Adm. Chuichi Nagumo, Rear Adm. Chuichi Hara, Vice Adm. Nobutake Kondo, and Vice Adm. Hiroaki Abe. Now and then a cool breeze would waft in through the portholes, giving a respite from the heat, but none dared to appear uncomfortable.

"Gentlemen," Yamamoto said, "as you know, the situation at Guadalcanal is desperate. Our troops are being decimated by superior numbers of American marines, the numbers of which we seemed to have underestimated. It's obvious that reinforcements must be forthcoming. This would be an easy task were it not for reports of American carriers southeast of Guadalcanal."

"How many carriers, sir?" Nagumo asked.

"At least three. I admit these reports are spread over a period of sightings and are not consistent, but we must assume the Americans have brought up carriers to cover their own troop runs." He glanced at each officer in turn before continuing. "Therefore, we are forced to do the same. Eighth Fleet cannot do the job by itself and we have lost precious ships in the process. Needless to say, Imperial General Headquarters is deeply concerned."

Yamamoto tapped a document before him. "This is Battle Plan KA. It defines our operations to be put into effect on the 23rd." He glanced at Nagumo. "Admiral, the carriers *Shokaku* and *Zuikaku* and screens are organized into Carrier Strike Force. Your purpose will be to seek out the enemy carriers and destroy them." To Hara he said, "Your command will be the *Ryujo* with the *Tone* and two destroyers, known as Detached Carrier Strike Force."

Nagumo was surprised. "The *Ryujo* is not to sail with the fleet carriers?"

"No," Yamamoto replied. "You will cover Admiral Tanaka's reinforcement flotilla carrying the Ichiki Detachment. Then you will strike the American airfield." Yamamoto pondered a moment, then continued. "Admiral Kondo, you will be in overall command of the Support Forces, with Admiral Abe commanding the battleships *Hiei* and *Kirishima* as the Close Support Group. You yourself will ride with the Vanguard Force with the seaplane tender *Chitose* and screen. The battleship *Mutsu* and three escorts will cover the fleet train. A standby force with the carrier *Junyo* will remain with me at Truk."

He leaned back wearily. "Any questions, gentlemen?"

Nagumo spoke up. "Sir, while my carriers are sufficient to destroy the enemy's, I cannot cover everything. Besides the *Ryujo*'s planes, will we get any land-based support?"

"Of course." Yamamoto straightened up. "As we speak, Admiral Tsukahara's Eleventh Air Fleet is replacing the depleted Twenty-Fifth Air Fleet at Rabaul. This force will repeatedly strike the airfield, joining up with *Ryujo*'s planes on her strike. Any more questions?"

There were none. Yamamoto got up, stepped to a porthole, and peered out at the sun-splashed waters. "You gentlemen know that my overwhelming desire has been to engage the American fleet in a decisive battle. We lost that chance at Midway, but we must not lose it again. Perhaps *this* time we will.

"You are dismissed. Take your sealed orders and return to your commands. We have much work to do and very little time in which to do it."

The officers silently rose, took their packets, and filed out, each glancing at their commander, who was still peering out of the porthole. Yamamoto's gaze shifted to the big carriers near Monday Island. "What I wouldn't give to have the *Kaga*, *Akagi*, *Hiryu*, and *Soryu* with me again." Then he turned to the closed door of his galley. "Zendo! Bring me some tea, please."[1]

On the morning of the 23rd, another commander in chief was pondering the situation at South Pacific Command Headquarters on Espiritu Santo. Like Yamamoto, Vice Adm. Robert L. Ghormley had been moving ships and supplies in an effort to reinforce his marines on Guadalcanal. Like those of Japan, his forces were operating on a shoestring and had to have supplies quickly. He was troubled by repeated reports of enemy ships gathering at Rabaul and Truk. A report of big carriers at the latter was especially disquieting. It meant the Japanese were planning a big move soon.

He glanced at his map of the Solomons as the plan unfolded again in his head. His carrier groups under Frank Jack Fletcher were Task Force 11, with the *Saratoga*; Task Force 16, with the *Enterprise*; and Task Force 18, with the *Wasp*. From New Caledonia and New Hebrides, Rear Adm. John S. McCain's patrol planes were sweeping around and to the north of the islands. At Henderson Field, the marines had twelve scout bombers and twenty fighters. Also available were thirty PBY patrol planes and thirty B-17s operating from South Pacific bases. He had a few submarines on the prowl.

Ghormley sighed. It wasn't much compared with what Yamamoto had. Besides numerous carrier planes, the Japanese also had unknown flocks of fighters and bombers at Rabaul. With his greater forces, Yamamoto could overwhelm him in an all-out scrap. But Ghormley had confidence in Fletcher, the conqueror at Midway, with his task groups operating 150 miles southeast of the Solomons, ready to counter any Japanese move.

Just then, Ghormley was told that a Japanese transport group with cruisers and destroyers had been sighted 250 miles northwest of Guadalcanal, moving at seventeen knots. Fletcher was taking action against it.

That's it, he thought. The enemy is making his move. The carriers are probably not far behind. Yamamoto wants a fight and, despite his superior forces, he'll get it! Remember who won the David-and-Goliath fight?

The bridge of the *Saratoga* was abuzz; reconnaissance reports were coming in from all over. Everyone knew something big was about to happen and tensions were high. Fletcher, a cold pipe in his mouth, sat in his chair, studying reports as they came in from land-based search planes and his own aircraft. Near him stood the *Sara's* skipper, Capt. DeWitt C. Ramsey.

"Three transports with screening cruisers of destroyers," Fletcher remarked. "A sizable invasion fleet, but not much protection."

"Probably part of a larger force," Ramsey replied. "No doubt bigger boys aren't far behind."

Fletcher glanced out of the port window. Towering clouds cluttered the sky and whitecaps danced over the ocean. The clouds were pretty but every carrier sailor knew that they could hide enemy dive bombers. He watched the crew preparing Dauntless SBDs and Grumman TBFs for takeoff. At least it was good flying weather.

"The big show will come from Truk," he said. "If Yamamoto is to engage us, his big carriers will sortie out from there. We must keep up our search sectors in the approaches from Truk."

"I'll turn her into the wind for launching," Ramsey said.

Fletcher thought about the ships he commanded. His flagship, all 33,000 tons of her, could make thirty-four knots and the 888-foot flight deck could launch all eighty-three planes in record time. She was an old girl, but a stout one. Launched in 1925, her keel originally was laid for a battle cruiser. She was among the largest carriers in the world and, with her late sister, the *Lexington*, was the mainstay of the Pacific carrier fleet.

The *Enterprise*, launched in 1936, was considerably smaller at 20,000 tons and 809 feet, but she too could make thirty-four knots and carried eighty-one aircraft. Her captain, Arthur C. Davis, knew how to handle her. The *Wasp* was even newer. Launched in 1939, she sported a 741-foot flight deck, displaced 14,700 tons, and carried eighty-four aircraft. She was ably commanded by Capt. Forrest P. Sherman. But Fletcher shuddered, as he regretted having to send her south for refueling when early reports had the Japanese carriers north of Truk. Where could that report have come from?

Fletcher glanced astern at his escorts, which included the newly arrived 35,000-ton battleship *North Carolina* and the light cruiser *Atlanta*, bristling with antiaircraft guns. A formidable group indeed, but he sorely missed the *Wasp*. Even though Admiral Ghormley had sent for the *Hornet* at Pearl Harbor, he doubted she would arrive in time for the showdown.

"So be it," Fletcher thought as a radioman handed him another report on the course of the Japanese group. There still were no signs of carriers or heavies of any kind.

Meanwhile, the "Big E" swung into the wind and launched eight SBDs to look for Tanaka's flotilla. Earlier, Lt. Stockton E. Strong and Ens. John H. Rickey had sighted an enemy scouting submarine and bombed it without effect. Still earlier, Lt. Albert Vorse had sighted a four-engine Japanese flying boat and shot it down. Many other planes and subs had been sighted and either shot down or sunk. The Japanese were scouting in earnest.

Fletcher was dozing when an excited radioman handed him a message. The admiral sat upright in his chair. At last!

Ramsey came over. "Important news, sir?"

"Damned right," Fletcher replied, handing him the message. "Patrols spotted an enemy carrier, one cruiser, and two destroyers bearing 317 degrees at 260 miles north by northwest of us. Signal Captain Davis to launch four Torpedo three planes to search out and destroy that carrier."[2]

On the bridge of the *Shokaku*, Admiral Nagumo also observed the good weather. As was Fletcher, he was concerned over those cumulus clouds. He ordered a sharp lookout lest American planes tumble out of them and lay "eggs" on his decks. He felt a shudder, remembering Midway, when the weather was similar. Never again would he be caught rearming planes on deck. Changing from bombs to torpedoes proved costly when the Americans got him with his pants down through clouds similar to these. As a result, he'd lost four fine carriers.

The two carriers he now commanded were splendid. The 26,000-ton *Shokaku* and her sister *Zuikaku* were newer vessels. Launched in 1939, the 844-foot *Shokaku* could hurl seventy-two planes into the air as well as twelve spares. Both ships could make thirty-five knots. They would be more than a match for their American counterparts. Once the U.S. carriers were gone, Kondo's battleships would mop up.

His musings were interrupted by a radio message. The *Ryujo* had launched six bombers and six Zeros to be met by planes from Rabaul for a strike against the American airfield on Guadalcanal. Another report indicated American carriers were still on a north-by-northwest course. Both fleets were approaching each other rapidly. At last he'd get a chance to avenge his defeat at Midway. He turned to the

*Zuikaku's* captain. "Prepare to launch planes to engage enemy forces."

Comdr. Tameichi Hara, skipper of destroyer *Amatsukaze*, one of the *Ryujo's* screen, was uneasy about the thirteen-year-old carrier. He knew that the best pilots were never assigned to older carriers. Midway had cost the navy many crack pilots and those aboard the *Ryujo* must be grossly inexperienced. The *Ryujo* was one of the emperor's oldest carriers. Launched in 1929, she was a mere 564 feet long, displaced 10,600 tons, and carried only forty-eight planes, twelve of which had been launched for the Guadalcanal strike. It worried him that there was no fighter coverage over her.

He also wondered whether the *Ryujo* was simply a decoy to draw American planes away from Nagumo's carriers. Even if that were true, there still was a job to do. He shook off his gloomy thoughts and ordered lunch to be brought to the bridge. He hoped he would get a respite.

He had just finished eating when a lookout reported enemy planes coming in from thirty degrees to port. He snatched up his binoculars and spotted a B-17 coming from the clouds, followed by a second. "Prepare to repel air attack . . . take evasive action!" He ordered a blast from the ship's siren and battle flags flung up the yard-arm. He glanced at the *Ryujo* and gasped. There was no reaction from her—no fighters on deck! They seemed to be asleep. What was the matter with Captain Kato?

"Commence firing!" he shouted, and the antiaircraft guns came alive, though the bombers were out of range. Again he glanced at the *Ryujo*. Two Zeros were taking off. At last, Kato had awakened. He wondered what Admiral Hara was thinking aboard the *Tone*. The destroyer skipper watched anxiously as the fighters scrambled aloft, but the B-17s had fled.

Angered and impatient, Hara sent a message to the carrier, asking his old friend Hisakichi Kishi, the executive officer, why flight operations were so laggard. It was impertinent, but he had to have an answer. It came swiftly. Kishi thanked his old friend for his concern, assured him of quicker action, and asked for his cooperation.

Hara snatched up his binoculars and watched as seven Zeros

appeared on deck and the carrier was turned into the wind. Excellent. Now we're getting somewhere.

"Many planes approaching!" a lookout reported.

Again the *Ryujo* was responding sluggishly. Her fighters were still on deck when the American planes tumbled down and straddled her with bombs. Hara watched in horror as two hit her stern. She burst into flames. More bombs and a torpedo slammed into her. Shortly, the carrier was running in circles, blazing furiously. Then the enemy planes headed for his ship, the flagship, and sister destroyer *Tokitsukaze*. It was their turn for a working-over.

"Hard right rudder!" he barked. "Commence zigzag pattern and commence firing!" Then the frantic cat-and-mouse game began; the swooping planes chased the zigzagging ships. The bombers had dropped their "eggs" haphazardly, simply splashing Hara's bridge. The *Tone* and the *Tokitsukaze* also appeared unscathed.

After the planes were gone, Hara anxiously searched for the carrier. She emerged from a thick cloud of smoke, then stopped and started sinking. A signalman called down the speaking tube from the flying bridge: "Flagship orders destroyers to stand by the *Ryujo* for rescue operations!"

"Left rudder!" Hara told the helmsman. "Head for the carrier." The task now, he thought, is to rescue survivors or tow the carrier back to Truk. He fervently hoped no more planes would appear; he wasn't sure how much more punishment the flotilla could take.[3]

Admiral Fletcher was bracing for trouble. A radar report indicated many "bogeys" at eighty-eight miles, bearing 320 degrees. He had also received word that Comdr. Don Felt's air group from the "Big E" had attacked the lone enemy carrier and her escorts; the carrier had been mortally hit, according to Felt. Another report informed him his planes had unsuccessfully attacked one of the big carriers to the north. Things were popping!

But Felt's planes were still aloft and far away when he needed them. Further, the radio channels were full of chatter from pilots. From the bridge speaker issued a mishmash of voices. Barely discernible were such remarks as, "Shift to high blower!" "Look at that one go down!" and "Bill, where are you?"

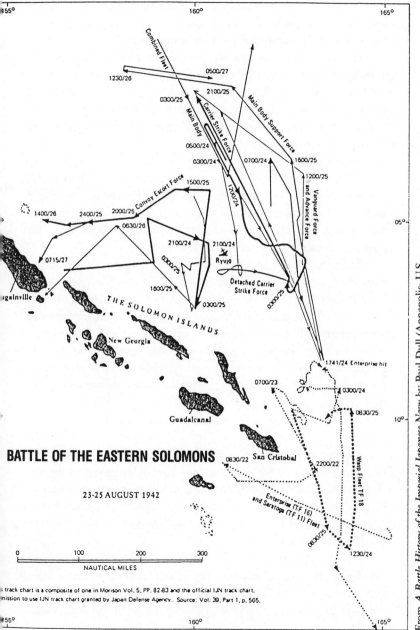

# BATTLE OF THE EASTERN SOLOMONS

### 23-25 AUGUST 1942

```
0        100        200        300
|————————|————————|————————|
        NAUTICAL MILES
```

track chart is a composite of one in Morison Vol. 5, PP. 82-83 and the official IJN track chart.
mission to use IJN track chart granted by Japan Defense Agency. Source: Vol. 39, Part 1, p. 565.

From *A Battle History of the Imperial Japanese Navy* by Paul Dull (Annapolis: U.S. Naval Institute, 1978).

Fletcher frowned. "How can I reach Don Felt through garbage like that? With the big Jap carriers coming on, I can't vector them to the attack. I'm betting we'll soon see some visitors."

He had formed his task forces into two groups ten miles apart with each carrier ringed by escorts. The *Enterprise* had two cruisers and six destroyers, plus the *North Carolina* 2,500 yards astern. The *Saratoga* had two cruisers and five destroyers. Twenty-five miles away was an umbrella of fifty-three Wildcat fighters; he had remembered a thing or two from Midway!

All eyes searched for enemy planes as the tension was as thick as a morning bowl of oatmeal; everyone knew the enemy was coming. The first sighting was from the destroyer *Monssen* of the "Big E" screen. Lt. (jg) George Hamm saw a flash of sunlight from the canopy of a Val. Soon, eight appeared in a straight line. The *Enterprise* saw them coming, too. The attack was on.

Zeros had kept the Wildcats from attacking the bombers. Fletcher ordered his gunners to open up as the first wave of Vals veered down the port side and port quarter, dropping bombs from 1,500 feet. The first hit the afterdeck elevator, penetrating to the third deck before exploding. A second hit near the first and a third hit just aft of the superstructure. The *Enterprise* was now burning furiously, and Captain Davis ordered all damage control crews into action. Concerned about the *Saratoga*, he radioed for a report and learned that her group was untouched. The *Saratoga*, he was told, had launched planes for a strike on the enemy task forces.

Unknown to Fletcher, a second wave of planes launched from Nagumo's carriers were searching for him. This group of eighteen dive bombers, nine torpedo planes, and three Zeros was panting for blood, but it changed course and missed Fletcher's ships. Had the Japanese found the "Big E" when she was most vulnerable, they would have finished her off.

Hara ordered his ship away. No sooner had she done so when the *Ryujo* groaned, rolled over, flashed her red bottom, and slipped beneath the surface. The suction made the *Amatsukaze* bob like a cork—it had been a close call! Among the survivors was Captain

Kato, who was a broken man. Hara was saddened that his old friend Kishi had perished with the ship.

It's a terrible thing to see a ship go down. You feel bad for the survivors, who look on helplessly as their home, workplace, and belongings plunge to the bottom of the ocean. It's sort of like watching your house burn down; it leaves a great sense of loss. When it's personal, you're only glad that you didn't go down with it, though many buddies did. Then there's the resolve to get another ship and get even with those who destroyed your home.

The *Enterprise* had been hit hard but not fatally. Damage control crews worked frantically to put out the fires and rescue men trapped below decks. Fire hoses were all around; emergency lighting cables were strung below.

Meanwhile, Admiral Kondo, whom Commander Hara described as a "British-gentleman sort of man," was having his own troubles. Two air groups from the *Saratoga*, led by Lt. Harold "Swede" Larson, had found him and were pressing the attack. Kondo ordered evasive maneuvers and narrowly escaped destruction. Then two American dive bombers, piloted by Lt. (jg) Robert M. Elder and Ens. Robert T. Gordon, found what they thought was an enemy battleship surrounded by its screen. Through heavy flak, they straddled the big ship with bombs, heavily damaging her. She was the 11,000-ton seaplane carrier *Chitose*. She was escorted back to Truk for repairs.

Commander Hara could hardly believe the *Ryujo* was still afloat as he maneuvered the *Amatsukaze* alongside the carrier's submerged starboard deck. There had been a brief alarm as three planes suddenly appeared; they were Zeros returning from the Guadalcanal strike. They circled the sinking carrier for a time, then ditched. The pilots were rescued.

Hara's fears increased when he glanced up at the carrier's superstructure, which, because of the rolling sea, was bobbing perilously close to his bridge. Some of the crew held the destroyer off with poles while the *Ryujo*'s crew slid long planks across to the destroyer's deck.

The wounded were brought across, followed by able-bodied crew members. The carrier lurched farther over. An officer called to Hara: "Sir, please cast off. This is getting dangerous!"

Many heroic feats were done that day to keep the *Enterprise* afloat. Among those recommended for the Navy Cross were Chief Machinist William A. Smith, who, after the carrier had lost steering control, plunged through smoke-filled compartments and restored it, though he was rendered unconscious a couple of times; Fireman 3/c. Ernest R. Visto, who led teams into the steering compartment and helped rescue survivors; and Carpenter's Mate Edward S. Clapp, who, at great risk, furiously tossed unexploded ammunition overboard, reducing that threat. There were many others, but these shining examples put their lives aside for their stricken shipmates. The *Enterprise* finally retired south for repairs.[4]

Shortly afterward, Admiral Kondo took his battleships and cruisers south, looking for American ships. He found none, then regrouped and retired to Truk. The battle of the Eastern Solomons was over. The casualty list included three Japanese ships sunk and two damaged against one crippled American carrier, which put a large hole in our fleet.

It's difficult to assess this carrier battle. The Japanese had won, having badly damaged one of the three carriers in the Pacific; the Americans had won because they had sunk three enemy ships, including a carrier, and had turned back a large-scale reinforcement attempt. But neither side really won. It was not the long-expected "decisive battle" with the American fleet, and the Japanese couldn't put large numbers of troops on Guadalcanal. Much of the blame rests with Yamamoto, who almost timidly committed carriers into battle without knowing the real strength of his opponent. Had he committed his entire surface strength, the results could have been very different. The United States had two carriers in the field (the *Wasp* had been sent south, unable to reach the combat area in time), and with the *Enterprise* disabled, only one carrier stood in the way of sweeping the Americans from the Solomons.

Kondo's halfhearted attempt to close his Vanguard Force of battleships and cruisers with the Americans was a waste of time. He should have known that the Americans didn't operate from carriers at night and were vulnerable to surface attack. Reports of the crippling of the "Big E" should have tipped him off.

On the American side, there was hesitation and, in some cases, confusion. While Fletcher's air groups were reaching out for the *Ryujo*, Nagumo's carriers had been spotted, but because of poor communications, he couldn't reach his pilots. Improved communications were sorely needed, since search planes and strike planes were on the same frequency. The senseless chatter had to be reduced. American commanders also had to beef up long-range reconnaissance flights. Carrier search planes' sectors were limited, so more land-based searches were needed. They also needed to adopt the Japanese tactic of using submarines for reconnaissance. The enemy carriers should have been spotted much earlier.

Finally, by sending the *Wasp* south for refueling after receiving far-away reports of Japanese carriers, Fletcher deprived himself of a carrier when he needed her. The crippling of the *Enterprise* took her away for repairs when she was needed most. Fletcher still had two carriers afloat, however, one of which could be used to ferry planes to Guadalcanal from bases in the south.

So it seems both sides had lessons to learn from this battle. Fortunately, we learned the most, as we shall see.

Although the Battle of the Eastern Solomons was primarily a carrier engagement, it is important in the story of the Tokyo Express. From that moment on, the Herculean task of reinforcing Imperial troops on Guadalcanal fell on the burdened shoulders of Admiral Tanaka and his remarkable destroyermen.

## NOTES

1. Hara. I am indebted to Hara for the reconstruction of this conference. Although he didn't describe this particular one, he did record others that had many of the same participants.

2. *Combat Narratives,* vols. II through VIII (Washington, D.C.: Office of Naval Intelligence, 1944–45). This is the primary source for accounts of the U.S. Navy's operations in the Pacific war. It was written shortly after the actions occurred and contains some errors and inaccuracies revealed by information gathered since. Therefore, it must be compared and checked with research from U.S. and Japanese sources. Still, it contains valuable data on ships, tactical maneuvers, battle groups, task forces, and the officers in command.

3. Hara, pp. 110–12.

4. *Combat Narratives,* vol. III, pp. 46–65.

# 9
# Aftermath of the
# Eastern Solomons

September 1942 was a mixed bag. With the carrier battle over, the hapless situations of American and Japanese troops on Guadalcanal, and the desperate reinforcement attempts by both sides, the situation deteriorated into a timid sparring match. The Guadalcanal struggle had burgeoned into something beyond what either side had envisioned.

That didn't mean things weren't happening. A continuous stream of ships flowed northward from Noumea, using Fletcher's carriers for protection, and the Japanese were still busy making Tokyo Express runs. The Imperial Army was of a one-track mind, totally absorbed in trying to take Port Moresby by way of the Owen Stanley Mountains of New Guinea.

Nevertheless, even hidebound generals usually know a bad situation when they see it. In late August, Lt. Gen. Haruyoshi Hyakutake sent 3,500 troops via the Tokyo Express. They neared Guadalcanal on the 28th and ran into a hornet's nest of dive bombers from the Cactus Air Force. The destroyer *Asagiri* was sent to the bottom and two more were damaged. The landing was called off and the shattered Express returned to Rabaul.

The next day, another "train" landed 450 soldiers on the island from the destroyer *Yudachi*. While covering this run, bombers spotted the fast U.S. transports *Colhoun* and *Little* busy landing supplies. The planes rained down a torrent of bombs that split apart and sank the *Colhoun*. More nightly Express runs put an additional 4,000 Imperial troops ashore.

Finally, the Imperial brass back-burnered the New Guinea operation and threw everything it had at Guadalcanal. Everyone knew a showdown was coming and the initiative seemed firmly in Imperial hands.

Meanwhile, the Americans suffered a setback on August 31. Admiral Fletcher's carriers *Wasp*, *Saratoga*, and *Hornet* were patrolling the lanes 260 miles southeast of Guadalcanal to protect convoys. Fletcher had to remain alert for any end run by the Combined Fleet to cover a large-scale landing. At 3:00 A.M., a submarine contact was made ten miles from the task force and carrier planes made an unsuccessful attack. Those concerned figured that it had to have been a rain squall on the radar screens, so the planes were recalled and the task force plodded on. At 6:00 A.M., breakfast was piped aboard the *Sara* and all hands settled down for a routine day. Unknown to them, the 2,500-ton submarine I-26 was watching from beyond the big carrier's screen. She launched six torpedoes. Despite a sub warning from a destroyer and evasive maneuvers, one hit the *Sara*'s starboard side, wounding twelve men, including Admiral Fletcher. She had to be towed back to Espiritu Santo for repairs. Ghormley had only two operational carriers left and the Japanese continued their Tokyo Express runs with impudence during September.

The first skirmish between the U.S. Navy and the Tokyo Express was on September 4 while the destroyer-transports *Little* and *Gregory* were landing troops and supplies on Guadalcanal. Unaware, the destroyers *Yudachi*, *Hatsuyuki*, and *Murakumo* were making a bombardment run. A Catalina flying boat pilot who spotted the gun flashes from the destroyers thought they were coming from a submarine, so he dropped some flares. Instead of lighting a sub, the flares put the American ships on center stage. The Japanese turned their guns onto the surprised Americans, who quickly swung into action, but their smaller-caliber guns didn't have enough range. The destroyer-transports were torn apart. It was another bad night for the U.S. Navy.

On September 19, a top-level conference was held at Noumea aboard Admiral Ghormley's flagship, the 19,000-ton auxiliary vessel *Argonne*. Ghormley was joined by Adms. Chester W. Nimitz and Richmond Kelly Turner; Gen. Henry H. "Hap" Arnold, chief of the Army Air Force; and other army and navy officers, including a representative from Gen. Douglas MacArthur.[1] It was agreed that if the Americans didn't do something soon, the Japanese would take back Guadalcanal.

The conference was called because of the loss of the *Wasp*. Ghormley had decided to reinforce Guadalcanal with the 7th Marine Regiment using six transports, covered by the *Wasp* and the quickly repaired *Enterprise* battle groups. On September 14, the task forces steamed from Noumea. The crews were on alert for submarines and planes. A Mavis flying boat was spotted, snooping around the fleet, and shot down, but it was apparent the Japanese knew the task forces were on their way.

At 2:00 P.M., the *Wasp* turned into the wind to launch planes. That was the moment the Japanese subs I-19 and I-15 had been waiting for. The I-19 fired four torpedoes, three of which hit the carrier on her starboard side. The fourth barely missed the destroyer *Landsdowne*.

The *Wasp* was devastated; planes were flung around, machinery ripped from its bases, and water mains broken. Captain Sherman ordered damage control crews into action, but the hits were lethal. She was burning from stem to stern and listing, already a dead ship.

The I-15 then fired a spread at the *North Carolina*, hitting the big battleship on the port bow. The damage was heavy but not fatal. One of the torpedoes struck the destroyer *O'Brien*, opening a gash in her bow, but fortunately she didn't burn.

When it became evident that the *Wasp* wouldn't make it, the crew was evacuated. The *Landsdowne* put five torpedoes into her, sending the new carrier to the bottom. It was a sad day for the Americans; another carrier was gone and a battleship and destroyer were damaged. The *O'Brien* was lost as she was being towed to Pearl Harbor.[2] Still, the marines and supplies were landed on Guadalcanal.

The situation was getting grim for the Americans in the Solomons. The Japanese still enjoyed superiority in all types of ships, especially carriers. The U.S. Navy now had only one carrier to ferry troops and supplies and to meet the Imperial Navy. The reports of a massive buildup of shipping at Rabaul and Truk were worrisome for headquarters. It was another sign that a showdown would come soon.

## NOTES

1. Samuel E. Morison, *The Two-Ocean War: A Short History of the U.S. Navy in the Second World War* (Boston: Little, Brown and Co., 1949); Samuel E. Morison, *The Struggle for Guadalcanal*, vol. 5 of *History of United*

*States Naval Operations in World War II* (Boston: Little, Brown and Co., 1949). Morison reports that MacArthur did not attend this conference, showing the division between the army and the navy at the time.

  2. Paul S. Dull, *A Battle History of the Imperial Japanese Navy: 1941–45* (Annapolis: Naval Institute Press, 1978). Professor Dull was a Japanese linguist and professional historian who spent twenty years compiling information from Japanese sources for this monumental work. It is the very latest and most authoritative piece on the Imperial Navy.

# 10
# Ripping the
# Cape of Esperance

To the south of Guadalcanal, the sun came over the eastern horizon, revealing a flotilla of American ships cruising off the formless, green clump of Rennell Island a few miles to the east. As usual, the Coral Sea was relatively calm and the soft trade winds were just beginning to stir. Scattered dumpling-like clouds floated across the incredibly blue sky of the South Pacific on October 11, 1942.

In his cabin aboard the heavy cruiser *San Francisco*, Rear Adm. Norman Scott studied notes, charts, and radio reports. He was putting the finishing touches on a plan for his Task Force 64. It was in response to sightings of enemy naval units in the Shortlands. He was ordered to destroy the ships and landing craft. The fifty-three-year-old admiral had no idea of the size of enemy forces, but reports from coast watchers and search planes indicated at least two "heavies" in the area. That could mean a real scrap.

He smiled slightly. His force consisted of his 10,000-ton flagship; the heavy cruiser *Salt Lake City*; two light cruisers, the *Boise* and the *Helena*; and five destroyers: the *Farenholt*, the *Buchanan*, the *Laffey*, the *Duncan*, and the *McCalla*. He checked off the plan: when the force entered Iron Bottom Sound, cruisers would launch floatplanes to scout the Guadalcanal shore for enemy landing craft and to drop flares and bombs. Then the ships would form a column with two destroyers in the van and two astern of the cruisers. If the enemy were spotted, the destroyers were to fire star shells and launch torpedoes. The heavy cruisers were to fire continuously against small ships, rather than use full salvos at long intervals. The remaining cruisers were to fire on his orders. The van destroyers were to keep TBS clear for orders and to use searchlights.

There! It was a combat plan figured out to every detail. It would be Savo Island in reverse, and this time he would have the initiative. He sat back and relaxed a bit. All he needed to know was the size and disposition of the Imperial forces.

A message arrived from ComAirWing at Guadalcanal. Search planes had located two enemy cruisers and six destroyers steaming down the Slot, 210 miles from Guadalcanal. Scott made some quick calculations. To intercept this force, his ships would have to reach Savo Island about 11:00 P.M. He was about to order the force under way when another message informed him that Henderson Field had been attacked by seventy-five planes in four waves. The four float-planes he had earlier dispatched to Tulagi would be unable to rendez-vous with his force in the sound, according to the plan.

When no further word came, Scott decided it was time to move if he were going to intercept that flotilla. He called to the bridge and instructed Capt. Charles McMorris to form a column and head for Savo. The column consisted of the flagship, followed by the *Boise*, the *Salt Lake City*, and the *Helena*. In the van were the destroyers in a 2,500-yard semicircle.[1]

On the bridge of a Savo Island veteran, the heavy cruiser *Aoba*, Adm. Aritomo Goto had relaxed for the first time since leaving the Shortlands. All day his force had been dogged by snooper planes, but he hadn't been attacked. It was 10:00 P.M. and darkness was his welcome ally. He knew no American ships would dare be off Guadalcanal and the Henderson Field planes never flew after dark. He checked his force; all ships were in place. His flagship was fol-lowed by the heavy cruisers *Kinusaga* and *Furutaka*, with two de-stroyers, the *Hatsuyuki* and the *Fubuki*, on his port and starboard beams, respectively.

His powerful flotilla protected a reinforcement group of two seaplane carriers, the *Chitose* and the *Nisshin*, with a screen of six destroyers. The ships were carrying a large part of the Second Divi-sion. By now the reinforcement group would be off Guadalcanal. He had to bombard the enemy airfield to cover the landings.

The *Aoba*'s skipper said, "Admiral, lookouts report flickering lights dead ahead."

"It could be the reinforcement group," Goto replied. "Answer them. Find out what they want." The signalmen tapped out a message to the light, but there was no response. They tried again; still no answer. This was reported to Goto. His search planes had reported no enemy ships in the area, so he concluded it was nothing important.

"Steady on course one-twenty-five degrees," he said to the *Aoba*'s captain.[2]

"Sir, the planes from Tulagi have appeared," Captain McMorris advised. "They've landed on the surface and request further orders."

Scott replied, "Slow column to ten knots and take them aboard. We'll launch later, when we approach the cape." He watched as a crane loomed out to take aboard the Curtiss SOC. Then he groaned when the plane was dashed against the side and heavily damaged. He quickly decided there was no time to salvage it, so he had the crew recovered and the plane scuttled by the *Buchanan*. Then the formation continued toward Cape Esperance.

When the force was thirteen miles from the cape, Scott ordered a scout launched from the *Salt Lake City*.

Bad luck prevailed; it caught fire from a defective flare and crashed. The crew survived but the flames acted like a beacon for a time. The admiral hoped that his surprise attack hadn't been spoiled. Surely lookouts from the Imperial ships would have alerted their captains.

Scott kept on course in a single column: the *Farenholt*, the *Duncan*, and the *Laffey* in the van followed by the flagship, the *Boise*, the *Salt Lake City*, the *Helena*, the *Buchanan*, and the *McCalla*. The night was like pitch punctuated by occasional flashes of lightning to the northeast—nothing unusual for the area. The lookout watch of the *San Francisco* weren't very concerned because they knew the "spinning bedspring" radar antenna atop the mainmast would spot any enemy ships in the Slot. It was a source of wonder, though none knew how it worked.

It is curious that Scott had chosen the *San Francisco* as his flagship, since she only had the SC, a long-distance air search radar. The *Boise* and the *Helena* had recently been overhauled and had the latest SG equipment. It was far more reliable for detecting surface vessels, though its range was limited to the horizon. Perhaps the admiral didn't fully grasp the potential of electronic gear. Also, the equipment in those days broke down often and had trouble separating targets from landscape clutter; this happened a couple of times in the Solomons battles. Parts were hard to come by because of radar's newness and there were few fully trained operators. This was soon to be corrected.

The radar fire-control equipment always seemed to work. It was short-ranged but extremely accurate and greatly offset the amazing vision of Japanese lookouts. Some ship captains preferred fire-control radar over their SGs and SCs.

Even we radar operators of that day felt the wonderment. It was an awesome responsibility, knowing that the safety of the ship and crew might rest on our shoulders. Consequently, radar men enjoyed a particular status with the rest of the crew. We were constantly pumped for information about sightings, but we couldn't talk about it, since we had been sworn to secrecy after radar school. In fact, the only other personnel allowed to see the equipment were the captain, the navigator, and the watch officer. No enlisted personnel were allowed in the radar shack.

Had others seen it, they would have wondered what the fuss was all about. They would have seen a console with three scopes and corresponding cranks. The larger scope contained a ribbon of light that, as it swept in a circle, revealed glowing dots on the screen as targets were spotted. A second scope contained a horizontal line of "grass" that resembled a short-bristled brush. When a "pip" appeared on the big screen, a pip shot up on the second. By rotating the crank, the operator lined up a steady pip below the line (the antenna) with the pip above the line. The distance appeared on the small scope in yards or miles. Bearings were read off the outer dial of the sweep scope.

Actually, it was a simple piece of equipment in those days but it meant the difference between life and death.

At 11:08 P.M., the *Helena's* radar made a contact at 27,700 yards, but it wasn't reported to the flagship until fifteen minutes later.

The cruiser's captain had been waiting to confirm the contact. A minute later, the *Salt Lake City* reported "three ships, range 16,000 yards." There definitely was something out there.

Then a scout plane reported, "Many enemy ships approaching Cape Esperance." This was it! Scott ordered a countermarch, which meant a 180-degree turn. The maneuver meant that the *San Francisco* would lead the column on the new course. The van destroyers, finding themselves in the rear, would have to race down the starboard side and take up the new van.

Like troops on a drill field, the ships swung about and resumed their new course southward. But fate wasn't ready to smile on the American force yet. The van destroyers had scattered and were ready to reassemble for the run down the main column. The *Duncan*'s fire-control radar had picked up a contact at four miles to starboard. Her skipper, Lt. Comdr. Edmund W. Taylor, glanced astern and saw that the *Laffey* hadn't swung about yet, so he assumed her captain, Lt. Comdr. Eugene T. Seward, had also picked up the contact and would join him in the attack. He rang up thirty knots and aimed his ship at the enemy. This was to be the first confusing action that night.

At 11:42 P.M., the *Boise* and the *Helena* reported contacts over TBS, and Capt. Robert C. Hoover of the *Helena* asked to open fire. Scott's answer was "Roger." This was Confusing Action No. 2. According to navy doctrine, Hoover's request was phrased, "Interrogatory Roger," meaning a request to open fire. Scott's answer was "Roger." "Roger" also meant "message received," which was Scott's meaning. In other instances, it could mean to commence firing. This was what Hoover thought, so he snapped on a searchlight and ordered his guns to blast away.

On the bridge of the flagship, Admiral Scott was startled when the night was torn apart by gun flashes. The *Salt Lake City* followed suit, as did the rest of the column, including the flagship. The gods were laughing now and it seemed someone else was in charge of things.

The *Aoba* came out of a rain squall at 11:40 P.M. and Admiral Goto cut speed to twenty-six knots. Everything had gone right for the Imperial Navy so far this night. No enemy ships were sighted and the seaplane tenders and escort destroyers were unloading their troops. Then a lookout reported three ships five miles dead ahead. Goto concluded they were members of the reinforcement group. After all, no enemy ships had been sighted anywhere near Guadalcanal.

Suddenly, the darkness was split asunder and his ship was hit hard. The *Helena*'s salvo had found the *Aoba*.[3] Goto ordered an immediate column right turn and the *Aoba* swung to starboard, followed by the *Furutaka*. But the *Kinusaga* and the destroyer *Hatsu-yuki* had, for some reason, turned to port. They must have misread his orders! After the *Aoba* turned, a shell hit the bridge and Admiral Goto was mortally wounded. Astern, the *Furutaka* was also hit hard, as was the *Murakumo*. The Japanese were in an intolerable situation.

With his ships firing steadily and making hits, Scott became worried that they were firing on the van destroyers, which should have been coming down his starboard side by now. He halted the firing and called to the destroyer division commander, Capt. R. G. Tobin, to report the location of his ships. Tobin replied that he was coming down the flagship's starboard beam. Scott said, "Flash recognition signals." The *Farenholt* and the *Laffey* (the *Duncan* was off to the north engaging enemy ships) flashed the standard vertical signal, green over green over white. Satisfied, Scott ordered his ships to resume firing.

The *Duncan* found herself in a hornet's nest. Alone, she had bravely charged an enemy contact, only to find herself between Japanese ships. A torrent of enemy and friendly shells fell around her and she was hit in the forward fire room. But she managed to fire her guns and get off torpedoes before enemy shells wrecked her gun director, knocked over her forward stack, and ignited powder in the No. 2 handling room. She veered off in flames with her coding and radar- and gun-plotting rooms smashed. Interior communications were gone and her decks were littered with dead. As flames reached the bridge, Lieutenant Commander Taylor ordered it abandoned. When it became evident the ship was doomed, he ordered her abandoned. After the wounded were taken off, the dying ship veered off in circles. She was the only U.S. ship lost in the battle.

At the same time, her sister *Farenholt* was hit, probably by American shells. Her rigging was destroyed, her port side holed, and her engine room hit. The crew kept her afloat by maintaining a boiler room and by shifting fuel and water. Also, the ship was purposely listed to starboard, raising the shell holes out of the water. Then she limped off toward Tulagi.[4]

The *Furutaka* was having her troubles. She started firing, then took heavy hits in return. By now she was aflame and mortally hit. Her action report states that she took hits in the No. 3 turret, No. 2

torpedo tube, and her port and starboard engine rooms. When her main battery was knocked out and engine rooms flooded, abandon ship was ordered. Capt. Kikunori Kijima, Admiral Goto's senior staff officer, found himself in charge after his superior fell. The situation still was not clear. He knew that the *Aoba*, followed by the *Furutaka*, had swung about 180 degrees and both had been punched by the enemy and were on fire. Where was the *Kinusaga*? Obviously, she didn't make the right turn. The *Hatsuyuki* and the *Fubuki* were nowhere to be seen. His first order was to strike back at his tormentors. The *Aoba*'s and the *Furutaka*'s aft guns were now uncovered and ready. "Commence firing!" he said.

On the *San Francisco*, McMorris's lookouts reported an unidentified ship a quarter-mile to starboard. She had been signaling unreadable characters and flashing obscure lights on her mast. Then she made a starboard turn. McMorris ordered a searchlight on. There, bathed in light with her white-banded stack, was the *Fubuki*. The *San Francisco* and the other American ships opened fire and the hapless destroyer exploded and sank.

Admiral Scott quickly assessed the situation. After realizing the enemy ships had reversed course and were now speeding away, he ordered a turn to the northwest, in order to parallel them. Now both columns were on a similar course.

The Japanese force, though badly damaged, still packed a punch. Several shells from the *Kinusaga* and the *Aoba* hit the *Boise* after she put a searchlight on an unidentified object. She careened away to the south, out of the fight. The glare from her fires illuminated the *Salt Lake City* astern and she received some minor hits.

The fight was not over. As the *Kinusaga* staggered on after lashing out at the American ships, Scott's vessels turned on her. She was now a floating bonfire.[5] It was now midnight and Scott called off the engagement. He set about gathering his force.

To the north, it was clear that the *Duncan* had to be abandoned. For a moment, beaching her on Savo Island was considered, but she couldn't make it. She was abandoned and after a brief salvage attempt by the *McCalla*, she sank at 3:00 A.M., seven miles from Savo. The shattered *Furutaka* had stopped twenty miles northwest of the island.

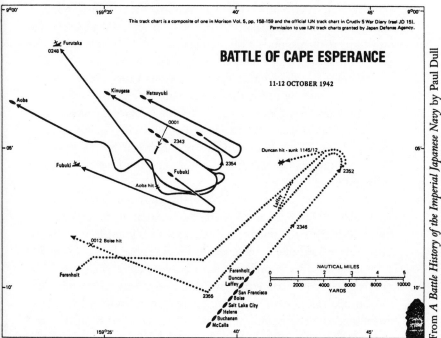

The *Hatsuyuki* came alongside and took aboard as many survivors as possible. It was none too soon; at 2:08 A.M., the cruiser turned turtle and went down.[6] The Battle of Cape Esperance was over.

This clearly was Scott's victory. His ships had crossed the enemy's T, sunk a heavy cruiser and a destroyer, and mauled a second cruiser. His force lost a destroyer and suffered serious damage to another and a light cruiser. He had accomplished his main objective—turning back this run of the Tokyo Express—but had not kept Goto from unloading troops and supplies. The Japanese considered it their victory in that though they lost four ships (two destroyers were sunk the next day by Cactus planes in the Slot as they looked for survivors), they had landed troops and artillery on Guadalcanal that were to give the American marines a rough time.

Many experts believed that Scott erred in having his ships in column, preventing the destroyers from using one bank of torpedoes effectively. It was a throwback to World War I, when warships marched in a column parallel to the enemy's and blasted away. The only ship to break out of this rigidity was the *Duncan*, when she dashed off to attack an enemy contact. It was a costly move.

In hindsight, the countermarch was a smart move because it put Scott in the position of "crossing" the enemy's T, a classic naval move that could have cost Goto his entire task force. But the countermarch also forced the vanguard destroyers to dash down in order to maintain their positions. This put them squarely between Scott's ships and Goto's, and no doubt caused the *Duncan* and the *Farenholt* to be hit by friendly fire.

It also would appear that Scott didn't fully appreciate his radar, especially the SG equipment. Fortunately, some of his captains did fully utilize their equipment, and the result was grievous for Admiral Goto. Scott's attitude is understandable, however, because few ship commanders had a complete grasp of radar's abilities. It was all so new, replacement parts were hard to come by, and there were few trained operators. All this was to change when radar schools were established in Hawaii and on the mainland. One last problem Scott had was the disquieting lack of discipline of his commanders, who ignored his cease-fire orders and acted on their own.

Much of the blame for defeat was Goto's. Convinced there were no enemy ships at Guadalcanal, he didn't have his crews at general quarters. As his force approached Guadalcanal, his guns were covered. He ignored the earlier report of the light coming from the burning U.S. scout plane. That should have alerted him, but still he blindly charged in. In essence, the Japanese juggernaut had been turned back to Rabaul, wounded and frustrated, as a result of the battle of Cape Esperance.

Admiral Tanaka commented later that Cape Esperance was a crushing defeat for the Japanese Navy. He noted that the American counteroffensives were getting "increasingly ferocious" and that the enemy's air power was growing stronger. He knew that trouble lay ahead for Japanese landing operations.[7] Still, Admiral Yamamoto wasn't tossing in the towel. He had his awesome Combined Fleet at Truk and he intended to use it.

# NOTES

1. *Combat Narratives*, vol. IV, pp. 6–26.

2. *Aoba* Action Report in *Tabular Records and Action Reports of Japanese Battleships and Cruisers.*

3. Ibid.

4. Roscoe, pp. 182–84. A detailed account of the damage and sinking of the American and Japanese destroyers.

5. *Kinusaga* Tabular Report in *Tabular Records and Action Reports of Japanese Battleships and Cruisers.*

6. *Furutaka* Action Report in *Tabular Records and Action Reports of Japanese Battleships and Cruisers.*

7. Tanaka. This penetrating chapter chronicles Tanaka's thoughts on the campaign as well as his strategy with the Tokyo Express.

# 11
# Encounter off the Santa Cruz Islands

The battle of Cape Esperance intensified the struggle for Guadalcanal. Though the Americans won, the Japanese were hardly rocked back on their heels. In fact, they were bold enough to initiate another major carrier battle that was to be the last of its kind in the Solomons. But there were two important preliminaries.

With Admiral Goto out of the ring, Vice Adm. Takeo Kurita took over and promptly planned a stiff blow at the hard-pressed Americans on Guadalcanal, especially Henderson Field. He knew that American ships had been cleared from the area because of the battle and therefore expected little or no opposition to his surface forces at night. Available to him were vessels including the 27,500-ton battleships *Kongo* and *Haruna*, older but powerful veterans of the Imperial Navy. The *Kongo* had been the first "modern" Japanese battleship built outside home yards. Though her two sisters were built in Japan, the navy ordered this dreadnought from the Vickers shipyard of Britain. She was built in 1912 and commissioned in 1913. The *Kongo* was not only for line use but also was an object of study for Japanese naval architects and engineers. Many of her features were built into future battleships. After modernization, she, like the *Haruna*, had eight fourteen-inch guns in four turrets with sixteen six-inchers in barbettes along her belt. She was among the finest and most formidable ships of her day.

Also available to Kurita were the new Type Zero shells with thin skins and a devastating burst. Both ships were equipped with 500 rounds of these incendiary projectiles.

On the night of October 13, Kurita brought the *Kongo* and the *Haruna* and their escorts to a point west of Savo Island and bombarded Henderson Field with 918 Type Zero shells for an hour. Planes, fuel dumps, and ammunition stores were pulverized and the remnants burned for twenty-four hours. The field was all but obliterated.[1]

One never forgets being on the receiving end of a naval bombardment. You crouch deep in your foxhole, wishing you could pull it in after you. You hear the door-like slam of a salvo at sea, the fluttering sound of the incoming projectiles, and the bone-jarring impact. Your body braces for the pummeling by dirt and debris and your heart beats so loudly you fear the enemy out yonder can hear it. You jam fingers in your ears to protect the drums and they ache for hours afterward. Most of all, you silently pray that none of the shells has your name on it. You wet your skivvies from fear but you're not ashamed because everyone else is doing it. Long after the bombardment is over, you crouch in the foxhole, fearful of being caught by a last salvo.

To add insult to injury, Kurita sent Admiral Mikawa out the next night with the heavy cruisers *Chokai* and *Kinusaga* to pound the field with 752 eight-inch shells, The effect was such that six Japanese transports unloaded troops the next morning in full view of the dazed survivors of "the Bombardment," as it was later tagged. That night, the cruisers *Maya* and *Myoko* sent in another 400 rounds.[2]

At Pearl Harbor, Admiral Nimitz was struggling with a decision about the command at Noumea. On the same night Mikawa's cruisers were churning up Henderson Field, he pressed his staff for an opinion on whether the indecisive Admiral Ghormley should be replaced. The unqualified reply was that he should be. Nimitz decided on his old friend, Adm. William Frederick Halsey, to take the reins at Noumea. Bull Halsey had just recuperated from a serious skin rash and was on a Pacific inspection tour before taking command of a carrier group. When he landed at Noumea, he received sealed orders that he was now in full command.[3]

This changed the picture in the Solomons. Halsey immediately ordered up a task force, including the new battleship *Indiana* from the Atlantic, the 25th Infantry Division from Oahu, fifty army planes, and a number of submarines. He was putting on the gloves and challenging Yamamoto to a fight. He wasn't about to let the Japanese commander get the upper hand. By the same token, Yamamoto wasn't going to give up the initiative—not by a long shot!

A spirit of unanimity had finally prevailed in the Japanese armed forces. Headquarters had decided on a two-pronged army-navy attack on American land, sea, and air forces in an effort to flush them from the Solomons once and for all. This had top priority, which was long overdue. Orders went out to Combined Fleet headquarters at Truk and to Lt. Gen. Masao Maruyama on Guadalcanal. The target date was October 22.

The plan was simple. The army would attack and occupy Henderson Field. Then the Combined Fleet, after standing off to the north of the Solomons, would move in, annihilate the American fleet in the area, and land carrier planes on the field. Everything hinged on Maruyama's taking the airfield, which just wasn't to be. After two nearly successful attempts, the Japanese were driven off by October 25 with heavy losses. This wrecked the plan and the Combined Fleet returned to Truk. The Americans had won this one and, what's more important, American marines had proven they could hold their own in jungle fighting.

Aboard the *Yamato*, flagship of Combined Fleet, at Truk, Yamamoto listened to the reports of fighting from Gaudalcanal. The enemy had many ships south of the island and an engagement was in the offing. He considered the odds: his four carriers, five battleships, fourteen cruisers, and forty-four destroyers were poised in several groups northeast of the Solomons against an American fleet of one or two carriers, three to five battleships, five to eight cruisers, and an undetermined number of destroyers. Some of his scouting reports were contradictory and he was puzzled over the carriers. How many did the Americans have? Where were they?

He was disappointed at the Japanese defeat at the airfield. What went wrong? Were Tanaka's destroyers still making reinforcement runs? More problems and questions. Then he decided: land victory or not, he'd seek out the enemy fleet and destroy it. He ordered Kondo to press forward and engage.

When Vice Adm. Nobutake Kondo, that "British-gentleman sort of man," received the word, he notified his task forces: Admiral Nagumo's Carrier Striking Force containing the *Shokaku*, the *Zuikaku*, and the *Zuiho* with one heavy cruiser and eight destroyers; Adm. Hiroaki Abe's Vanguard Group of the battleships *Hiei* and *Kirishima*, plus two heavy cruisers, one light cruiser, and seven destroyers; Admiral Kurita's Close Support Group with the battleships *Kongo* and *Haruna* with six destroyers; and Adm. Kakuji Kakuta's Second Fleet Air

Group with the light carrier *Junyo* and two destroyers. Kondo's own Advance Force was made up of four heavy cruisers, one light cruiser, and six destroyers. He also had 200 planes, twelve submarines, and Mikawa's cruisers and destroyers from Rabaul. His mighty fleet was more than well prepared to take on the Americans.

Kondo had reason to be proud and confident. His ships were in superb condition, his flyers were the best in the world, and ships' crews were highly trained and able to meet all contingencies. He would move in for the kill.

Halsey also was aware of the odds, but he too had a powerful force. President Roosevelt himself had ordered him to hold Guadalcanal and had pledged that all possible weapons would be placed in his hands. Halsey had two battle groups: Task Force 16, with Rear Adm. Thomas C. Kinkaid commanding with the carrier *Enterprise*, the battleship *South Dakota*, two heavy cruisers, and eight destroyers; and Task Force 17, with Rear Adm. George D. Murray commanding the carrier *Hornet*, two heavy cruisers, two light cruisers, and six destroyers. Backing these groups was Rear Adm. Willis A. Lee with the new battleship *Washington*, two heavy cruisers, two light cruisers, and six destroyers. Unfortunately, Lee's formidable force was too far away to take part in the action.

Halsey put down the dispatches, turned to his aides, and ordered the following message to be sent to the fleet: "Attack . . . Repeat . . . Attack!" It was a welcome rallying call for the fleet.

Round One was about to begin. It was October 24.[4]

At 5:30 A.M. on October 25, a search plane from the cruiser *Tone* sighted an American task force 200 miles north of the Santa Cruz Islands and reported it to Nagumo aboard the *Zuikaku*. He knew that an attack was imminent. He glanced at the sky and was dismayed by the cumulus clouds—those potential hiding places for enemy planes. Then he thought about how his flight crews were on a high state of alert and that a combat air patrol was on the job. He relaxed a bit.

Yamamoto had Admiral Abe's battleship force in the vanguard sixty miles south of Nagumo's carrier force; Kondo's Advance Force was off to the west, guarding the carriers; and farther west was

Admiral Kakuta's *Junyo* group. By placing Abe's force in the van, Yamamoto hoped to draw American carrier planes to it and spare his carriers. There was a ring of destroyers and a cruiser around the three carriers. Nagumo, remembering Midway, was taking no chances. They were well protected this time.

At Truk, Yamamoto was aware of the American carriers and quickly ordered Nagumo to reverse course. He desperately needed more information. How many carriers were there? Fearing that indecision would accomplish nothing, he ordered the strike force south again at 6:00 P.M.

On board the *Enterprise*, Admiral Kinkaid studied reports from his scout planes. He knew there was a large Japanese force to the northwest but had only sketchy information about it, and no carriers had been spotted. The game of hide-and-seek was in full swing and the fleets were being drawn inexorably toward each other. At 6:50 A.M. October 26, Lt. Comdr. James Lee and Ens. William E. Johnson spotted Nagumo's carriers. Before they could attack, they were driven off by the combat air patrol.

First blood was drawn at 7:40 A.M. Two American search-and-destroy planes came upon the same carriers and attacked. A bomb hit the *Zuiho*'s stern, wrecking the flight deck and putting her out of action. Meanwhile, other planes of the *Enterprise* search group found Abe's force and attacked, but missed the *Tone*. American luck was beginning to run out.

At 7:55 A.M., Nagumo lashed out at the elusive American carriers, which finally had been pinpointed by one of his cruiser search planes. He launched sixty-two planes and prepared a second strike of forty-four.

The Americans hadn't been asleep. At 7:30 A.M., seventy-three SBD dive bombers, Avenger torpedo bombers, and Hellcat fighters had roared off the *Enterprise* and the *Hornet* toward Nagumo's force. On the way, these air groups passed their Japanese counterparts headed in the opposite direction. The airmen gaped at one another but, for some reason, didn't engage. A following group from the *Enterprise* wasn't so lucky. Twelve Japanese fighters peeled off and downed three Wildcats and three Avengers, losing only two of their

A night battle in a Solomon Islands campaign.

Rear Adm. Raizo Tanaka, IJN, "father" of the Tokyo Express.

Fleet Admiral Isoroku Yamamoto, commander in chief, Combined Fleet.

This rare photo shows two U.S. warships hit by torpedoes in the Solomon Islands struggle. The carrier *Wasp* is in her death throes in the background, while in the foreground the destroyer *O'Brien* receives a direct hit.

The USS *Patterson* (DD 392), veteran of the battle of Savo Island.

The USS *Quincy* (CV), sunk in the Battle of Savo Island.

The IJN *Kirishima* (BB), which was sunk in the second battle of Guadalcanal.

Vice Adm. Gunichi Mikawa, IJN, commander of Eighth Fleet.

Rear Adm. Norman Scott, USN. Victor of the battle of Cape Esperance.

The IJN *Atago* (CV), veteran of Solomon Islands campaigns.

The IJN *Jintsu* (CL), Admiral Tanaka's flagship.

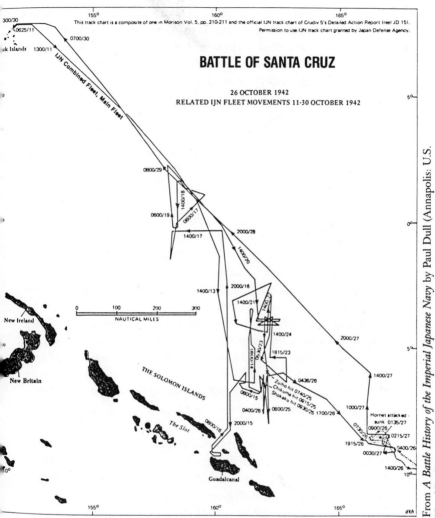

BATTLE OF SANTA CRUZ

26 OCTOBER 1942
RELATED IJN FLEET MOVEMENTS 11-30 OCTOBER 1942

This track chart is a composite of one in Morison Vol. 5, pp. 210-211 and the official IJN track chart of Crudiv 5's Detailed Action Report (reel JD 15). Permission to use IJN track chart granted by Japan Defense Agency.

From *A Battle History of the Imperial Japanese Navy* by Paul Dull (Annapolis: U.S. Naval Institute, 1978).

own, but the Americans warned their fleet comrades about the oncoming enemy. It was a momentous event—two large air groups were headed for each other's carriers.

The Japanese arrived at 8:40 A.M. They saw a tight formation: the *Hornet* surrounded by the heavy cruisers *Northampton* and *Pensa-*

*cola*, the light cruisers *San Diego* and *Juneau*, and six destroyers. What they didn't see was the *Enterprise* surrounded by the battleship *South Dakota*, the heavy cruiser *Portland*, the light cruiser *San Juan*, and eight destroyers. They were ten miles away, hidden in a rain squall. The Japanese also didn't know about the thirty-eight patrol fighters ready to pounce upon their Zekes, Vals, and Kates. Alas, these fighters were too high and too far away to intercept the enemy planes.

Momentarily defenseless from the air, the American ships flung up a curtain of antiaircraft fire, but it wasn't enough. Streaking bombs from the Vals hit the *Hornet* on the starboard side of the flight deck. Others buckled plates on the hull. The *Hornet* had been hit badly. Then a Val, badly damaged from antiaircraft fire, dove kamikaze-like into the superstructure, then glanced off and plunged through the flight deck, its bombs exploding in the bowels of the ship. Then the Kates sent torpedoes ripping into the engine rooms, bringing her to a stop. More bombs rained down, penetrated the deck, and exploded deep within. Another suicide dive blew up the forward elevator shaft. The *Hornet* was burning all over.

While the *Hornet* was being pounded, Lt. Comdr. William J. Wildhelm, leading her air group of twenty-one bombers and torpedo planes, came upon Nagumo's carriers at 9:25 A.M. They were jumped by nine Zeros. A dogfight ensued, during which two American escorts were shot down. The bombers pressed on and put four 1,000-pound bombs on the *Shokaku*'s flight deck, knocking her out of action for six months.

On board the destroyer *Amatsukaze*, Lt. Comdr. Tameichi Hara watched the attack. He was dismayed that four bombs could put the big carrier out of action. He wondered why she was so vulnerable, with her crack pilots and efficient crew. His musings were cut short by orders for him to rush to protect the *Zuikaku*.[5]

Still another *Hornet* air group found Abe's force and worked over the cruiser *Chikuma*, putting her out of action for a time. They attacked the *Tone* unsuccessfully. In another sector at 10:40 A.M., an *Enterprise* air group found Abe's ships and attacked but missed the battleship *Kirishima* before they were driven off. The Americans had fired their last shot. Two Imperial carriers were intact and Nagumo was determined to finish off the *Hornet* and find the elusive *Enterprise*.

The "Big E" got into action at 11:05 A.M. when she emerged from the squall in time to meet Nagumo's airmen. She was hit by bombs twice but dodged a spread of torpedoes from the *Junyo*'s planes. The *South Dakota* was hit by a bomb on the forward turret, killing one man and wounding fifty. Imperial airmen then turned their attention to the light cruiser *San Juan* and holed her with an armor-piercing bomb, but she stayed afloat.

The attack was nearly over. The *Hornet* seemed to be in a better position now; her fires were out and lines were sent out to the *Northampton* with hopes of towing her back to Espiritu Santo. For a time it looked as if the *Hornet* would be saved, but at 3:20 P.M., planes from the *Shokaku* and the *Junyo* torpedoed the wounded ship. The carrier was dead in the water again. Fortunately, most of her crew had been taken off at 2:40 P.M.[6]

The destroyers *Mustin* and *Anderson* were left behind the retreating fleet with orders to sink her. Sixteen torpedoes and heavy shellfire failed to kill the proud carrier. The destroyers had to abandon her because of reports that Kondo's force was closing. The destroyers *Makigumo* and *Akigumo* were the first to reach the burning hulk. After realizing she was beyond salvaging, Kondo ordered them to send her to the bottom. It took four more torpedoes.

For a time, Kondo picked up the scent of the U.S. task forces and swept southward, but was unable to make contact. He gave up after Yamamoto ordered him to Truk with the rest of the fleet. The battle of Santa Cruz was over.

This carrier battle was hard to call. Judged by sunken tonnage, the Japanese won. The United States lost the *Hornet* and the destroyer *Porter* (she was sunk by a submarine during the battle) and suffered damage to the *Enterprise*, a battleship, a heavy cruiser, a light cruiser, and a destroyer. This left Halsey with just one damaged carrier in the area. The Imperial Navy suffered heavy damage to the carrier *Shokaku* and moderate damage to the light carrier *Junyo*, a heavy cruiser, and two destroyers.

Still, the Japanese plan failed. When the army failed to retake

Henderson Field, Nagumo's planes couldn't fly in and occupy it. Much more serious was Yamamoto's loss of many seasoned pilots, reducing the effectiveness of his remaining carriers.

Once again, poor communications hampered U.S. air operations. Early in the encounter, reports of enemy ships were long delayed, preventing Kinkaid from making the first strike. The new 40mm antiaircraft guns on the battleship and cruisers didn't stop the Japanese from destroying the *Hornet* and damaging other ships. It wasn't until 1943, when the new Bofors guns were extensively fitted onto American ships, that this weapon took a terrible toll of enemy planes.

The Japanese had their weaknesses as well. Kondo's hesitation and his failure to close with the crippled, retiring Americans killed the last chance to mop up Halsey's fleet and drive the marines from the Solomons. His timidity was to later cost him his command at sea. Captain Hara of the *Amatsukaze* wrote later that the strategic victory belonged to the Americans because it bought regrouping time. The cost was minimal because Kondo was "lacking in spirit," he said.[7] Had Kondo been more aggressive, the damaged *Enterprise* might have been sunk, as well as other ships.

No matter how the pie was sliced, much of the blame was Admiral Yamamoto's. He again split his forces, as he had done at Coral Sea, Midway, and the Eastern Solomons. Historians agree that had he flung the bulk of the Combined Fleet at the Americans when they were most vulnerable, after the Eastern Solomons, the course of the war would have been very different. Some have ventured that his battleship mentality always took over.

Maybe his loss of 100 planes convinced him to withdraw, though he still had two operational carriers. It's inconceivable that he didn't know American carrier strength in the South Pacific had been drastically reduced. When he had a chance for that decisive fleet action at the Eastern Solomons and again at Santa Cruz, why didn't he consolidate his fleet and press forward?

We will never know because he didn't have a chance to write his memoirs. He was killed on April 18, 1943, when his plane was shot down over Bougainville. The Americans had received intelligence of his inspection visit there, and sixteen P-38 fighters were dispatched from Henderson Field to intercept his flight. His plane and an escort were sent flaming into the jungle. It was a real blow to the Japanese, who regarded him as a hero and a conqueror.

Because of the time the Americans bought at the battle of Santa Cruz, no heavy reinforcements of Imperial troops were landed on Guadalcanal, the enemy had been driven back on land, and the airfield was still in U.S. hands. More ships and planes were on their way to the South Pacific and American airmen and seamen got a breather. Still, both sides were determined to hold Guadalcanal and a showdown had yet to come.

At Truk, a fuming Yamamoto ordered the Tokyo Express back on track. He was already gathering powerful forces there and at Rabaul for another reinforcement attempt. The most savage surface battles in modern history were at hand.

## NOTES

1. *Haruna* Action Report in *Tabular Records and Action Reports of Japanese Battleships and Cruisers*. The *Haruna* reported "entire enemy field set afire." True enough, but a puzzling entry states, "Enemy raised white flag to indicate surrender." Of course, there was no such action.

2. *Chokai, Kinusaga, Maya*, and *Myoko* Action Reports and Tabular Movements in *Tabular Records and Action Reports of Japanese Battleships and Cruisers*.

3. Potter, *Bull Halsey*, pp. 157–60. Upon receiving this new command, Halsey's reaction was, "Jesus Christ and General Jackson! This is the hottest potato they ever handed me!" The same account is found in Potter, *Nimitz*, p. 198.

4. Potter, *Nimitz*.

5. Hara, p. 131.

6. Morison, *Guadalcanal*, pp. 221–22.

7. Hara, p. 152.

# 12
# First Toe-to-Toe
# off Guadalcanal

The tropical sun beat mercilessly on the decks of a transport tied alongside a pier in the spacious harbor of Noumea. Another transport was moored on the opposite side. Both were taking on troops and supplies. In the shade of the promenade deck of the 10,000-ton former liner *Santa Barbara*, now the USS *McCawley*, two soldiers talked. The burly sergeant took a cigarette and handed one to the corporal.

"Sometimes I wish I was back in Minnesota," said the sergeant, lighting both cigarettes. "*That* weather's halfway human. This South Pacific is for the birds."

"Aw, it ain't bad," replied the corporal. "Not for me, anyway. I'm from Arizona." He blew a puff of smoke. "Where in hell we goin', Sarge?"

The sergeant glanced around before answering. "We're gettin' a briefing at sea, but I don't see any harm in telling you." He waited until some soldiers had passed, then lowered his voice. "We're heading for a place called Guadalcanal. They say the marines are gettin' their butts kicked by the Japs. Looks like it'll take this man's army to bail them out."

"Must be a big push, Sarge. Look at all them ships in the harbor." The sergeant glanced out at the huge harbor now shrunken by anchored ships. "The Navy'll fight our way there, for sure. They say Jap ships are all over the place." He jerked a thumb toward the bridge. "That's old Admiral Turner's job up there. Him and Bull Halsey will get us through."

On the bridge, Adm. Richmond K. Turner watched the loading of the army's 182nd Reinforcement Regiment onto his flagship. He wasn't as optimistic as the sergeant about getting the men and supplies to the marines safely. Besides the 182nd, he had to land the 245th Field Artillery Battalion and other army and marine units on Guadalcanal. Two large transports, the *President Adams* and the *President Jackson*, also former liners, were loaded and ready to depart. Around them was part of Task Force 67, under Turner's command, consisting of the heavy cruiser *Portland*, the light cruiser *Juneau*, and four destroyers. They would escort the transports.

To the north at Espiritu Santo, Rear Adm. Daniel Callaghan's two segments of Task Force 67 were awaiting orders. He had two heavy cruisers, one light cruiser, and six destroyers; the second segment, under Rear Adm. Norman Scott, was composed of a light cruiser, four destroyers, and three cargo vessels loaded with aviation supplies and personnel. Nearby cruised a carrier task force with the *Enterprise*, the battleships *South Dakota* and *Washington*, two cruisers, and eight destroyers. These forces showed Halsey's determination to reinforce Guadalcanal.

Turner glanced over at the other transport at the pier, the *Crescent City*, and saw that she was almost loaded. Good. Time was short. At a last-minute conference with Halsey, the plan was finalized: after an air sweep of the Guadalcanal area, Task Force 67 was to sail from Noumea on November 8, followed by Callaghan's group from Espiritu Santo on the 9th and 10th. All forces would join and head to Guadalcanal for landings on the 12th.

Halsey was worried about reports of heavy units north of the Solomons. They indicated that Yamamoto had two to four carriers, two to four battleships, a lot of destroyers, and eight to twelve transports. Increased air activity indicated that Henderson Field might be bombed, followed by surface bombardment at night. A major enemy landing attempt was possible on the 13th.

Halsey and Turner agreed that it was imperative the transports be unloaded before then. Then Callaghan's ships would scout Savo Sound, ready to meet any forces coming down the Slot. Turner frowned. He knew he was outweighed and outgunned, especially if battleships were involved. He also suspected that Halsey would be reluctant to commit his last carrier unless the situation became grave. He shrugged. It was David and Goliath again.

The loading was completed; he'd now get the show on the road. The task force got under way at 3:00 P.M. on Sunday, November 8, 1942.[1]

Much farther to the north, another anchorage was bustling. Steady streams of captains' gigs shuttled to and from the battleship *Hiei* in the Shortlands. Eight destroyers and the light cruiser *Nagara* had steamed in from Truk that morning and their skippers were getting last-minute orders from Admiral Abe, commander of a bombardment group made up of the *Hiei* and her sister, the *Kirishima*, plus the cruiser and eleven destroyers.

This attempt meant business. Poised to the north of the Solomons was Admiral Kakuta with the carrier *Junyo* and support vessels, ready to support the reinforcement run by Abe's ships and a flock of loaded transports. The army had decided to commit the 38th Division to Guadalcanal. The entire unit was landed without opposition by twenty of Tanaka's destroyers from November 2–10.

But enemy air activity was growing and headquarters decided that Henderson Field must be rendered useless. Abe and his group were to boom down the Slot and bombard the field with his battleships' fourteen-inch guns before another run at the island by the transports. The gathering at the Shortlands was to be a super Tokyo Express indeed!

Replenishment complete, the task force set out for Guadalcanal at 8:00 A.M. November 9. The *Hiei* and the *Kirishima* were in the center behind the *Nagara* with destroyers in an arc ahead of her. Another half-ring of five destroyers was spread out in the van. When the force came within twenty miles of Guadalcanal after midnight, a severe rainstorm engulfed it and made all hands nervous, except for Abe, who looked upon it as a blessing. It would protect him from air and surface opposition. But in such a tight formation, navigation was difficult in the storm. Only superb seamanship prevented collisions.

One of the *Hiei*'s seaplanes was launched and promptly reported that there were no enemy ships off Lunga Point. The storm had swept over the entire area. Realizing that his ships couldn't bombard in such weather, Abe ordered a countermarch with speed reduced to twelve knots. He was taking no chances of running aground. The rain stopped at 1:24 A.M.

"All ships turn 180 degrees!" he ordered. The force was back on track, but his destroyer rings had broken up; the van ring was now in separate groups. He was now twelve miles from his target. The main batteries on the two battleships made ready.

In the early morning on the previous day, Scott's ships stood off Lunga Point unloading supplies. The weather was calm and the sky dotted with clouds at 10,000 feet. Everything was going smoothly. At 9:20 A.M., the unloading was halted and Scott ordered his ships out of harm's way. Enemy planes had been reported heading down the Slot from Rabaul. Ten bombers and fifteen fighters attacked. Most were shot down by the *Atlanta* and marine fighters from Henderson Field. Some of the transports were damaged, but Scott returned to Lunga Point and resumed unloading.

The radio room of the *San Francisco* was buzzing. Reports from coast watchers and Admiral Scott's force were pouring in. They could have meant an imminent naval battle. Turner's force had been joined by Callaghan's and was approaching Indispensable Strait, the southern approach to Guadalcanal.

Turner was particularly anxious about reports of enemy battleships in the Solomons. In a showdown, his cruisers would be hopelessly outclassed. He glanced at the two forward eight-inch gun turrets and knew they could do a job on a battleship at close range, but that was the trick, wasn't it? He shrugged. The enemy may have bigger guns, but he had faith in American ingenuity and seamanship.

First, though, the transports must be brought in and their vital cargoes unloaded. At 5:30 A.M. Thursday, November 12, they were off Kakum Beach and the warships formed a ring around them. All went well until enemy bombers were reported. Turner ordered the force away from land and into antiaircraft readiness. Some of the Bettys skimmed the surface at fifteen feet but were driven off. The ships moved back toward land and unloading was resumed.

At 10:35 A.M., a scouting plane had spotted Japanese ships moving down the Slot. "Two battleships or heavy cruisers, one heavy or light cruiser, and six destroyers; distance from Guadalcanal, 335 miles," the pilot reported.[2] At 10:45, five destroyers and a *Natori*-class cruiser were sighted 195 miles north of Santa Isabel Island.

Turner noted that since they had no transports, the groups must be on a bombardment mission. Against them he had two heavy cruisers, a light cruiser, two antiaircraft light cruisers, and eleven destroyers. He assigned all the cruisers and eight destroyers to Callaghan and took the transports south. Once they were safe, Callaghan formed his ships into a column: the *Cushing* was followed by the *Laffey*, the *Sterett*, and the *O'Bannon*; then the light cruiser *Atlanta*; the flagship *San Francisco*; the heavy cruiser *Portland*; the light cruisers *Helena* and *Juneau*; and the destroyers *Aaron Ward*, *Barton*, *Monssen*, and *Fletcher*.

The sound was moonless at midnight with a calm surface and a breeze from the southeast. After sweeping the Savo Island area and finding nothing, Callaghan once again set a northeast course, headed for the Slot.

At 1:30 A.M., a radar man aboard the *Helena* gaped at his scope. He saw three groups of targets: the first at 27,100 yards, the second at 28,000 yards, and the third at 32,000 yards. He reported it to the bridge and Capt. Samuel P. Jenkins reported it to Callaghan. This report was relayed to the commander by TBS, because the flagship did not have SG radar.

On the bridge in the pagoda mast of the *Hiei*, Abe was studying reports from his observers on Guadalcanal. The storm had abated and no enemy ships were off Lunga Point. Very good. The bombardment would proceed. He had had one-ton Type E incendiary shells stacked in the turrets of the battleships. He had sixteen .45-caliber fourteen-inch guns loaded for bear.

The cautious Abe was disturbed over his ships' placement since the two 180-degree turns. They had broken up his tight arrangement. In the van were the destroyers *Murasame* and *Yudachi*, followed by the cruiser *Nagara*. On her starboard quarter were three destroyers flanking the battleships. Strung out on the starboard beams of the *Hiei* and the *Kirishima* were six destroyers in a ragged column. The neat admiral had decided to re-form his column when the bridge radio cackled, "Enemy sighted!" This was from the *Yudachi*.

Abe demanded to know where the *Yudachi* was and the range of the bearing. Before he could find out, a *Hiei* lookout reported four ships to starboard at 8,700 yards. Abe ordered the incendiary shells replaced with armor-piercing ones. During this time, any hits his battleships took could turn them into infernos. His ordnance crews flung themselves into a flurry of activity in the turrets and in the magazines. Luckily, Abe got eight precious minutes to replace the ammunition. He was ready for a fight.

Callaghan called for more information after the *Helena*'s initial radar report. Subsequent sightings from the *Helena* and *O'Bannon* indicated that some of the enemy ships were heavies and they were bearing down on the Americans. Callaghan swung the column northward. He was hoping to cross the enemy's T as Scott had done at Cape Esperance. Then everything fell apart. The abrupt change threw the ships into disarray; the *Atlanta* swung left to avoid hitting the *O'Bannon*, which was turning to avoid ramming the *Sterett*. The column broke up and the van destroyers were thrust between two Japanese columns.

Not a shot had been fired. Desperately, Callaghan ordered the column to form up, but it was too late and his call wasn't heard by some ships; there was too much jabbering on TBS. Then he ordered, "Stand by to open fire! Odd ships fire to starboard; even, to port!"

Then the Japanese drew first blood. The *Akatsuki* and *Hiei* flicked on searchlights and pinned the *Atlanta* in cones of light. Captain Jenkins ordered the searchlights shot out. His guns responded, and the *Akatsuki*'s light went out. Before the *Atlanta* could zero in on the *Hiei*, the leviathan had turned and opened up with all eight guns at 4,500 yards. White-hot fourteen-inch shells tore into the luckless cruiser. Her superstructure was demolished and almost all hands on the bridge, including Admiral Scott, were killed. A torpedo slammed into her and she reeled off, a dying ship.[3]

Then began a saloon brawl in which it was every man for himself. The battle was so confusing that it is difficult to reconstruct the maneuvers. Only individual ships' action reports can give an idea of the action. The next ship to be knocked out was the *Barton*, tenth in line. Upon hearing Callaghan's firing order, she swung about to launch fish. Suddenly, she had to stop to avoid a collision. Then two torpedoes broke her in two and she sank almost immediately, taking most of her 250-man crew with her.

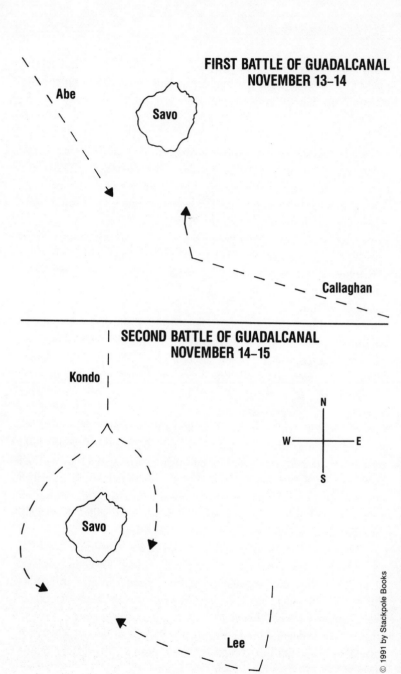

**FIRST BATTLE OF GUADALCANAL**
**NOVEMBER 13–14**

Abe

Savo

Callaghan

**SECOND BATTLE OF GUADALCANAL**
**NOVEMBER 14–15**

Kondo

Savo

N
W — E
S

Lee

Meanwhile, Abe was blinded and confused. His ship was being paid back for using searchlights, as was the *Akatsuki*, which was battered to a pulp in a crossfire between the *San Francisco* and the *O'Bannon*. The *Hiei* was staggering under the impact of American shells, but Abe composed himself long enough to order his ships to retire.

The *San Francisco* swung her guns and began blasting away. To his horror, Callaghan realized he was shooting at the *Atlanta*. He halted the firing. It was now 1:55 A.M. Suddenly, projectiles started pounding the *San Francisco*. The *Kirishima* had come up from the rear and, with support from two destroyers, concentrated on the American flagship. The *San Francisco*'s bridge was demolished, Admiral Callaghan along with it. The Americans had lost two admirals in a matter of minutes.

On board the *Amatsukaze*, Captain Hara saw the *Hiei* repeatedly hit by American fire. Some of the shells cascaded around his own ship. He watched as the mighty flagship spewed flames from her rugged mast. Then, intending to punish the enemy, he ordered a torpedo run on an unidentified American ship. He and his crew watched with satisfaction as the fish spread out and tore the vessel in two. That was the *Barton*.[4]

The *Cushing* and the *Laffey* were about to strike and be struck. The *Cushing* was the first to sight the enemy and, after missing a chance at the destroyers that cut across her bow, plunged in among the mass of ships, launched torpedoes, and then was pounded. Several Japanese shells hit amidships and crippled her. While she was fighting fires and trying to restore operations, the *Hiei* suddenly loomed on her port beam. Too close! Torpedoes glanced harmlessly off the steel plating of the towering battleship, which by now had swung to port. Meanwhile, the *Cushing* had stopped and immediately became pinned by enemy searchlights. She was almost blasted out of the water and her skipper ordered her abandoned. She sank the next day after losing fifty-nine men.

The *Hiei* had made a wide swing to the south and reversed course to the northwest. As she plowed along, long flames flowed from her battered mast; she had been hit repeatedly by the American cruisers and destroyers and was staggering. As she did, she found herself on a collision course with the *Laffey*, which had followed the *Cushing* into the center of the enemy column. The *Laffey*'s skipper, Lt. Comdr. William E. Hank, made a sharp turn to avoid a collision. He fired two torpedoes at her, but they bounced off because there was not enough range for them to arm themselves.

The *Hiei* crossed the stern of the *Laffey*, so close her wake rocked the destroyer. The *Laffey*'s gunners, taking advantage of the range, streamed 20mm and machine gun rounds into the pagoda superstructure, killing her skipper and slightly wounding Admiral Abe. As the dreadnought passed, her aft turrets pounded the *Laffey* to shreds. That and a torpedo hit astern sank the destroyer almost immediately.[5]

The sound to the east of Savo Island contained the deadly free-for-all. Gun flashes lit the sky like a gigantic fireworks display; tracers flew back and forth; here and there, a ship erupted into a white-hot ball of fire while others reeled along, trailing fire and smoke. Huge geysers reached skyward from near-misses while star shells hung lazily in the sky, casting a hazy, dancing light over ships while shells whizzed in to reduce them to wrecks.

The *San Francisco*, battered and helpless, her skipper and Admiral Scott dead, drifted in the center of the melee. She became the focus of Captain Hara's *Amatsukaze*. The destroyer launched torpedoes and raked the dying cruiser with five-inch shells, setting her afire. Then Hara decided to aid the *Hiei*, but she was too far away. As he swung about, he saw the destruction of the destroyer *Yudachi*, which had been pulverized by the *Aaron Ward*.

Suddenly, his own ship came under fire from port. The *Helena* had come up and was prowling for targets. Shells splashed around Hara's ship and two hit, knocking out the hydraulic system. With manual rudder control, the *Amatsukaze* limped away, trailing smoke. This seemingly indestructible ship made it back to Truk.

The *Helena*'s Captain Hoover, thinking he'd finished off the *Amatsukaze*, looked for other targets, but he came under fire from three destroyers in Abe's van that, during the battle, had fallen to the rear of the column. The *Asagumo, Murasame,* and *Samidare* pulverized the cruiser, putting her out of action for a long time. Captain

Hara reported that an unidentified destroyer approached the three Japanese ships and, thinking they were friendly, flashed recognition lights. This was fatal. Within minutes, her deck was torn up, her bridge demolished, her fire and engine rooms wrecked, and all power gone. She was later identified as the *Monssen*, lost with 130 of her crew. Callaghan's once-powerful force was now a shambles.

The *Hiei*, her skipper dead, Admiral Abe wounded, and almost immobilized, tottered along drunkenly. There were more than fifty hits in her superstructure and turrets. All around her were burning or sinking ships of both sides. The destroyer *Yukikaze* was escorting her to the safety of the north end of Savo Island. Finally, she was dead in the water. The destroyer began taking off her crew. To the northwest, the *Kirishima* and the *Nagara* were fleeing for home, accompanied by the remnants of Abe's force.

The entire struggle, so heavy with death and destruction, had taken thirty-four minutes!

The sun came up over Savo Sound on the 13th. The glassy surface was dotted with debris, burned-out hulks, and crippled ships. Among them were the *Portland*, her steering gear gone; the *Aaron Ward*, dead in the water; the *Atlanta*, the *Cushing*, and the *Monssen*, all charred; and the fire-ravaged *Yudachi*, dead on the surface. The *Portland* stirred for a time and sank the *Yudachi*, but it was a waste of shells. Her crew had been taken off during the night.

To the north of Savo, the *Hiei* also came to life after hearing the gunfire in the sound and sent off a salvo from her aft turrets. All this did was attract marine fighters from Henderson Field. She was hit by bombs and torpedoes all day but refused to sink. At 6:00 P.M., a destroyer took off the remaining crew members, but not until her sea cocks were opened. She was the first Japanese battleship sunk in the war.

Back in the sound, Navy tugs were herding out the *Portland* and *Atlanta*. The *Portland* was towed to Tulagi while the *Atlanta* was nudged to Lunga Point. It had been another bad night for the U.S. Navy.

One more act was played out in this drama. The ravaged *Juneau* and *Helena* and the badly damaged *San Francisco* and *Sterett*, accompanied by the undamaged *Fletcher*, had retired southward. These cripples were moving at a dangerously slow speed. They didn't know that the submarine I-26 had been shadowing them, waiting to strike. Suddenly, a spread of torpedoes was flung at the flotilla. One missed the *San Francisco*, the main target, but another passed under her keel and struck the *Juneau*'s port side. The ship disappeared in a ball of fire and a rain of debris within twenty seconds! Because of the sluggishness and an ineffective sub screen, no rescue attempt was made; it was assumed that no one survived. Actually, a few made it to Santa Catalina Island, but more than 700 crew members perished with the cruiser.

At the first battle of Guadalcanal, the Americans lost two light cruisers and four destroyers, and two heavy cruisers, one light cruiser, and three destroyers were damaged. Two of their admirals died. The Imperial Navy lost a battleship and two destroyers, and four destroyers were damaged. Short as it was, the battle was one of the most vicious in modern naval history.

Many interesting facts and conclusions may be drawn from this battle. Tactically, the Japanese decimated the U.S. force with their superior gunnery and torpedo techniques. Strategically, the Imperial Navy was again thwarted and Henderson Field was intact. Also, the loss of the *Hiei* left an unfillable hole in its battle line. The Japanese mistakenly assumed that the Americans wouldn't attack a superior force. Fortunately, U.S. confusion allowed Abe time to replace the bombardment ammunition with armor-piercing shells and his destroyermen distinguished themselves with their use of torpedoes. The Americans still didn't seem to have the knack. The Americans had lost, tactically, because of their heavy losses in ships and men, but it was a strategic victory in that it turned away Abe's bombardment mission. The losses seriously pared U.S. naval forces in the South Pacific, however.

Serious defects blunted the American response to Abe's challenge. Perhaps the most important was the lack of TBS coherency during the battle. Here's an example from the *Helena*'s TBS log:

2:00 A.M.: *To CTF (commander task force) from Helena:* Your course, please.

*To Helena from CTF:* Would like your course.

*To Portland from CTF:* Request your course.

*To any ship from Helena:* Can you hear?

*To Helena from Monssen:* Affirmative.

*To Portland, CTF, Juneau, and Atlanta from Helena:* Course, please.

*To Portland from Helena:* Please answer.[6]

Still, even the most helpful report would have had difficulty getting through on a ship-to-ship network that was cluttered with useless inquiries and dubious information. As in the battles of the Eastern Solomons, Cape Esperance, and Santa Cruz, the commander was stymied by the lack of information coming in and the inability to get his information out. For example, it took eight minutes for Callaghan to get the *O'Bannon*'s report of enemy destroyers dead ahead. It was all Abe needed.

All in all, this round went to the U.S. Navy for taking the heat off Henderson Field. Nimitz was moved to write, "Had the powerful enemy fleet succeeded in his mission of bombarding our airfield on Guadalcanal, the task of preventing a major enemy attack and landing of large-scale reinforcements would have been much more difficult, if not impossible."

The Japanese weren't through. They considered this battle a minor setback. At Truk, Admiral Yamamoto gathered more resources for another try at reinforcing Guadalcanal. They included a big transport force from Bougainville, Mikawa's heavy cruisers at Rabaul, and Admiral Kondo's force of a carrier, two battleships, nine cruisers, and thirty-eight destroyers. The Japanese commander in chief would open Round Two of this continual naval battle in the calm waters of Iron Bottom Sound. The U.S. Navy was about to be plunged into another life-and-death encounter.

## NOTES

1. *Combat Narratives*, vol. V, pp. 4–7.
2. Ibid., p. 14.

3. Unfortunately, the *Hiei*'s records are missing from *Tabular Records and Action Reports of Japanese Battleships and Cruisers*.

4. Hara, p. 144. Hara contradicts all other published accounts of this battle. He says Abe *was* expecting an enemy surface attack.

5. Roscoe, pp. 194–95. The destruction of the *Laffey* and the *Monssen* is chronicled in detail.

6. *Combat Narratives*, vol. V, p. 76.

# 13
# Repeat Toe-to-Toe off Guadalcanal

For some unexplained reason, Admiral Yamamoto had an aversion to committing the full strength of his awesome naval power against American forces entrenched in and around Guadalcanal, as exemplified in the battles of August through November 1942. The celebrated admiral was highly revered in Japan and among Imperial forces because of his brilliant planning and execution of the attack on Pearl Harbor and the successes of Combined Fleet in the ensuing months. During that time, it had spearheaded Japanese conquests to the south and southwest, in the first phase of the "Greater East Asia Co-Prosperity Sphere."

Curiously, the defeat at Midway was never held against him — at least during his lifetime. One reason for this may have been that the Japanese people never learned of the debacle until after the war was over and Yamamoto was but a memory. His reputation remained untainted except to historians.

But Yamamoto's predisposition toward flinging forces piecemeal against the Americans while hoarding the mighty Combined Fleet has puzzled historians. His actions are reminiscent of the tactics used by Maj. Gen. Ambrose Burnside, who in his effort to destroy Confederate forces at Fredericksburg on December 13, 1862, repeatedly flung his soldiers against a Confederate stronghold across the Rappahannock River and suffered staggering losses. Burnside, meanwhile, was safely ensconced at his headquarters in the city. Yamamoto's efforts were much like that futile effort, the primary difference being that the Japanese commander in chief, unlike Burnside, didn't use the full power of his forces.[1]

Yamamoto flung limited amounts of ships and planes against his own wall of Guadalcanal while directing the battles from Truk, many miles away. It would appear that he never actually understood the real importance of the Solomon Islands to his country's cause.

But, like Burnside, he refused to give up, and after the routing of his naval forces on November 13, he decided to press on. He had already alerted Admiral Kondo and his Bombardment Group, along with Admiral Tanaka and twelve loaded transports supported by Mikawa's cruiser division, to be ready to go up against the wall again.

"Tenacious" has been used to describe Tanaka's efforts, but it could just as easily be used to describe Yamamoto. The reasons are clear: time was running out; his navy was being whittled down by attrition; and Japan's supply of oil was getting low so Imperial directives directed fuel conservation. Therefore, Yamamoto had to move quickly. He decided on a plan that would be successful and also boost the morale of his forces. It was a move that had worked before. Mikawa would take the cruisers *Chokai*, *Suzuya*, and *Maya*, accompanied by the light cruiser *Tenryu* and two destroyers, into Savo Sound and churn up Henderson Field.[2] On November 15, this force hurled 1,730 rounds at the airfield. The shelling was ineffective but it gave Imperial forces a shot in the arm.

On the way back to Rabaul, after this group was joined by the rest of Kondo's force, which had been screening to the west, the flotilla was caught in open water off New Georgia by *Enterprise* planes and aircraft from Henderson. The *Kinusaga* was hit in her forward gun mount and heavily damaged by near-misses. She had repaired the damage and corrected her list when more dive bombers appeared and worked her over. She went adrift and sank later fifteen miles from Rendova Island.[3] The *Chokai*, the *Maya*, and the *Isuzu* also were hit, the last by a crash-dive that damaged her forward guns and a torpedo tube. Thirty-seven men were killed. The *Isuzu* and the *Maya* had to be towed back to Rabaul.

Yamamoto still had plenty of big ships to thrust into the fray. He assembled a bombardment group with the battleship *Kirishima*, the heavy cruisers *Atago* and *Takao*, the light cruiser *Nagara*, and two destroyers. A "sweep force" under Admiral Shintaro Hashimoto consisted of the light cruiser *Sendai* and the destroyers *Urnami*, *Shikinami*, and *Ayanami*. These two groups were to rush in and bombard Henderson before a landing of troops by Tanaka's eleven destroyers and eleven high-speed transports.

Backing all this would be the main body support force with the battleships *Kongo* and *Haruna*, the heavy cruiser *Tone*, and two destroyers. And as if that weren't enough, the "mobile force," built around the carrier *Junyo*, would be standing by to the north. It was to be a powerful thrust, one that Yamamoto hoped would drive the Americans from the Solomons.

At Noumea, things were in high gear. Halsey was determined to stop the enemy thrust. He fired off dispatches to Admiral Kinkaid, commander of Carrier Task Force 16, built around the *Enterprise*. Kinkaid was to keep the force south and send Task Force 64, with Rear Adm. Willis A. "Ching" Lee and his new battleships *Washington* and *South Dakota*, along with four destroyers, to Savo Sound to battle Kondo's force. Halsey still seemed reluctant to commit his last carrier because her damage from Santa Cruz was still being repaired, at sea.

Lee was a dyed-in-the-wool battleship sailor and knew how to use his fast ships and their advanced radar gear. Lee was made a captain in 1936 and was to become a vice admiral in 1944. He was chief of staff for the commander in chief of the Pacific Fleet before being appointed commander of a task force in February 1942. He was savvy and just the man to go up against Yamamoto's battleships in the Solomons.

His ships were superb. The flagship, *Washington*, of 35,000 tons, was 700 feet long, 108 feet wide and sported eight sixteen-inch guns, ten five-inch secondary guns, and nine five-inch antiaircraft guns. The *South Dakota* was heavier and wider and carried more secondary guns. No wonder Lee was confident of taking on Kondo's battlewagons!

Early evening found Task Force 64 west of Savo Island. At 9:30 P.M. on November 14, it swung eastward to a point eleven miles north of Savo, where Lee received a report of an enemy cruiser and destroyer hiding in a cove there. The report was unfounded. No such ships were in Savo Island harbor. He formed a battle line with the van destroyers *Walke*, *Benham*, *Preston*, and *Gwin* 300 yards apart, with the *Washington* and the *South Dakota* 5,000 yards astern. At 10:48, the force turned south and east of Savo toward Lunga Point.

About the same time, Kondo brought his sizable force toward Savo from the north. According to tradition, he split his ships. The *Sendai* and her escorts were sent to the northeast of Savo and the destroyers *Ayanami* and *Urnami* headed along Savo's western side. It was Kondo's pincer movement to trap any enemy ships in the sound.

About 11:20, a sharp lookout on the *Sendai* spotted Lee's force about five miles to port on a southeasterly course. These ships were reported as being heavy cruisers.[4] None of the Japanese was expecting two American battleships in the area. Kondo immediately sent the *Nagara* and four destroyers directly south so they could pass around Savo's west side and ambush the Americans. He kept his battleship, two heavy cruisers, and two destroyers north of Savo and swung south to enter the sound.

When radar picked up enemy ships west of Savo, Lee changed course to almost due west. Curiously, he wasn't aware that he was being shadowed by the *Sendai* all this time. The two forces were on a collision course. Though Kondo tipped the weight-and-guns scale, he didn't have Lee's two huge battleships.

At 12:05 A.M., the *Washington's* radar picked up the *Sendai* and her escorts at 16,000 yards and began tracking them until they became visible about five minutes later. This was the moment Lee had waited for. At last, after much maneuvering and countermaneuvering by the combatants, the dark, oppressive night in Savo Sound was about to be fractured by gunfire.

The *Washington's* sixteen-inchers bellowed at the *Sendai*, 11,000 yards out. The *South Dakota* joined in. Geysers shot up around the cruiser and the destroyer *Shikinami*. The *Sendai's* skipper turned sharply to the north and ordered smoke.[5]

Meanwhile, Lee's van destroyers spotted the *Ayanami* and *Urnami* as they swung around Savo. Immediately, the *Walke*, the *Benbam*, and the *Preston* fired at the surprised Japanese. North of the destroyers, the *Nagara* and her four consorts were on a parallel course and were sighted by the *Gwin*, which opened fire. The Japanese recovered quickly. All five Imperial destroyers responded with gunfire and torpedoes. The *Gwin* was hit hard, her engine room smashed. She stopped temporarily and was able to continue steering only after the *Washington* imposed herself between the *Gwin* and the enemy destroyers.

Savo Sound was now filled with gunflashes, exploding star shells, and burning ships. Like schools of barracudas, Long Lances were everywhere. One hit the *Walke*, which had previously been crippled by gunfire. Her B turret was flung away and the forecastle disintegrated. She sank immediately with seventy-five of her crew. Then the *Preston*, third in line, was pounded by five-inch shells. The *Nagara* had approached virtually undetected and opened up on the destroyer. All seven of the *Nagara's* five-inchers were concentrated on the *Preston*, which rolled over, her bow pointing at the sky for ten minutes before she sank with 112 of her crew.

The *Nagara* turned her guns on the *Benham*, next in line. She too was mauled and had to retire. The *Nagara* had hit fast and hard.[6]

The Japanese hadn't gotten off free. All this time, the destroyer *Ayanami* had been pounded by enemy shellfire. She drifted off and was scuttled that morning. Meanwhile, Kondo, with blood in his eye, was thundering southward with his big ships. Lee was busily watching him on radar. With the destroyer phase of this battle over, it was time for a struggle between battleships. After a brief exchange with what the *Washington* thought were batteries on Savo Island, she turned her attention to Kondo's big ships.[7] Unfortunately, at 12:03 A.M., the *South Dakota* lost power fore and aft and was temporarily out of action. She swung to starboard as the *Washington* swung to port to avoid crippled destroyers.

This maneuver caused the battleships to lose contact (the *South Dakota's* TBS was out), which Lee didn't know. It also affected the coming duel with the *Kirishima* because it brought the *South Dakota* close to Kondo and his searchlights. Japanese destroyermen quickly spotlighted the American battleship and the *Kirishima's* fourteen-inch batteries pounded her. The *South Dakota* lost her radar gear, gun directors, and fire-control systems. Her fuel compartments were punctured and she suffered thirty killed and sixty wounded. The battleship retired southward with more than forty hits.

Strangely, the pounding of the *South Dakota* served as a diversion. The *Kirishima's* gunners were so absorbed with her that they didn't know that the *Washington* had come up on a parallel course 8,000 yards away. Her sixteen-inch batteries quickly scored at least three hits and "large clouds of black smoke and steam poured forth, followed by flames."[8] The *South Dakota* sent salvos from her aft guns as she retired.

The *Kirishima* reeled off, rapidly taking on water.[9] "Fire broke out in all compartments. Considerable flooding occurred and steering became impossible." The cruisers *Nagara, Takao,* and *Atago* had also been hit and were forced to retire.[10]

Both Kondo and Lee ordered their forces to retire. The two combatants limped away from the arena, leaving behind four ships on the bottom and suffering damage to six more.

The *Kirishima* lived only a short time. After survivors were taken off by her destroyers, she was scuttled at 3:20 A.M., 7.5 miles from Savo Island. Her action record optimistically claimed that she had sunk a large cruiser and a battleship.[11]

The second battle of Guadalcanal was over. It was a savage, costly engagement for both sides. The Japanese had lost another battleship and a destroyer, the United States three destroyers and a battleship so damaged she had to be sent home for repair. For the entire November 13–15 fighting, the Japanese lost two battleships and three destroyers, with four destroyers damaged; the United States, two cruisers and seven destroyers, with one battleship, two cruisers, and seven destroyers damaged. Neither nation could afford such losses.

The Japanese pressed on. What was left of Admiral Tanaka's convoy of eleven transports, scheduled to land the 38th Division on Guadalcanal, was ordered to continue toward the island after a bombardment by Mikawa's cruisers grounded enemy planes. The Combined Fleet brass planned on Kondo's battleships and cruisers finishing the job Mikawa started, that of eliminating the Cactus Air Force.

Tanaka left the Shortlands on the night of the 13th with his transports in four columns, ringed by destroyers. Around dawn, he was attacked by B-17s and carrier-based planes temporarily based at Henderson Field. The convoy was unscathed, but in the late afternoon, forty-one planes sank two transports and damaged a third so badly that she had to turn back.

Troubles piled up for Tanaka. Less than two hours later, eight B-17s and five carrier bombers roared in and sank two more transports. He was now down to six transports, but that was soon to change. At sunset, twenty-one American planes zoomed in and sank another. Though 400 men from the 38th Division had been killed, most of the soldiers had been rescued by destroyers.[12]

Tanaka was spared even greater losses by the second battle of Guadalcanal. He had been ordered by Yamamoto to continue with his remaining transports, to be covered by the Kondo force. When the first shots of the battle were fired, Tanaka retired to the Shortlands.

The intrepid admiral sat patiently in his cabin aboard the *Hayashio* in the Shortlands harbor. When word was flashed that the *Kirishima* had been fatally damaged, he felt misgivings about the success of the landing operation. How could he bring his ships to Guadalcanal without air or sea cover? He would only have his destroyers. Surely Combined Fleet headquarters would hold off on any more moves until heavy units could be brought down from Truk. Then, on the 15th, he received the dreaded message to unload the remainder of the 38th Division on Guadalcanal. The *Hayashio*, followed by the transports and the destroyers upon which the survivors of the sunken transports had been loaded, steamed out to sea.

The way down the Slot was free from attacks, but the delay of his departure worried Tanaka. Since his vessels would reach Tassafaronga Point in daylight, planes certainly would attack them, assuming the ships were unloaded with lighters and barges as usual. Tanaka sat on the darkened bridge of the flagship, turning the problem over in his mind. Then it hit him: *why not run the ships aground?* He sat upright. It would work! Once the ships were aground and the troops over the side, the supplies could be unloaded directly by the ships' booms. He asked the commanders of the Second and Eighth fleets for permission. Eighth Fleet refused but Second Fleet told him to go ahead.[13]

At 2:15 A.M., he ran the transports hard aground on the beaches. Using nets, the troops climbed over the sides and waded ashore while the booms swung out and lowered the supplies. But the Americans on Guadalcanal were aware of this audacious move and, after sunup, scrambled bombers and fighters while B-17s winged up from Espiritu Santo. The planes reduced the transports to piles of junk.

Later the same day, the destroyer *Meade*, a recent arrival from the states bristling with 40mm guns, steamed up and down the coast and pulverized two beached transports that somehow had escaped the bombing. One was at Tassafaronga and the other at Doma Cove. The *Meade* then strafed the beaches with 40mm shells, killing many Japanese soldiers. Meanwhile, Tanaka had gathered his destroyers and scooted up the Slot to the safety of the Shortlands.

It had been two bad days for the Imperial Army and Navy. The attempt to reinforce their Guadalcanal garrisons had failed. Only 2,000 of the original 10,000-man 38th Division made it and eleven precious transports were lost.

The second battle of Guadalcanal ended in a Japanese rout. Over three days, the Imperial forces lost two battleships, a heavy cruiser, five destroyers, eleven transports, and 5,000 soldiers. Never again did Yamamoto stage a large amphibious operation in the area. In fact, American reconnaissance flights revealed a sharp decrease in shipping in the Shortlands following the battle. A captured enemy pilot disclosed that the heavy bombardment squadrons at Rabaul had been halved. The U.S. conclusion was that the Japanese expected major attacks on their bastions, but that would have been difficult because of recent American losses.

It was the beginning of the end for Japan in the Solomons. There would be one more sea battle, but it was inevitable that Japanese troops would be withdrawn from Guadalcanal and eventually from the entire chain. For some reason, Yamamoto was still hesitant to commit his major warships all-out against the Americans. All that stood in his way was a carrier and some damaged smaller ships. His reasons died with him.

The U.S. Navy had learned well from the battle. Radar had been used more intelligently and, in spite of Lee's battle line, the destroyers made individual torpedo runs, which may have contributed to the death of the *Kirishima*. He was able to report that, because of fire-control and SG radar, "the long range at which we opened fire and the accuracy of our initial salvos, fired without artificial illumination, must have been a distinct surprise [to the enemy.] . . . SG permitted our ships to navigate with some confidence at high speed in restricted and unfamiliar waters when visual and optical ranges were unobtainable."[14] However, Lee's fear of Japanese searchlights was realized when the *South Dakota* wandered off course, was pinned by the beams, and pounded by large-caliber shells. His concern was a distinct nod to this Japanese talent.

Admiral King wrote that, in spite of heavy losses, the United States had gained the upper hand in the Solomons and was never again seriously threatened by the Imperial Navy there, though the Tokyo Express landed small quantities of supplies and equipment from time to time. He knew that control of the sea and air had passed to the United States.[15]

Lee also improved TBS. It was to be used only for radar contacts and action reports. There was no more chitchat on TBS from then on.

After the two battles, the Imperial Navy wanted to evacuate and consolidate forces in the northern Solomons. The army rejected the proposal and ordered more reinforcements. As a result, the Tokyo Express, as King had mentioned, would be back on track. Already, "Tenacious" Tanaka was assembling destroyers in the Shortlands and loading them to the gunwales with troops and supplies. This run was scheduled for November 29. Little did he know he would spark the final surface battle in the southern Solomons—one that would bode ill for U.S. Navy forces in the area. The goal was Tassafaronga.

## NOTES

1. Edwin P. Hoyt, *Yamamoto, the Man Who Planned Pearl Harbor* (New York: McGraw-Hill, 1990), p. 225. Hoyt points out that Yamamoto was realizing his greatest fear, the burgeoning productive capacity of the United States.

2. Yamamoto felt confident his cruisers would be unopposed because reports told him the American battle fleet had retired southward after the night battle of November 12–13. Indeed, Halsey had done so.

3. *Kinusaga* Action Report in *Tabular Records and Action Reports of Japanese Battleships and Cruisers*. This account states that it was the second

attack that sealed the *Kinusaga*'s doom. The engines and steering were gone and "flooding became uncontrollable."

4. *Sendai* Action Report in *Tabular Records and Action Reports of Japanese Battleships and Cruisers.*

5. Ibid. The following entry is terse and to the point: "Enemy fired on us . . . laid down smoke and diverted enemy in order to decoy enemy to our main strength." Obviously, her skipper hoped the American "cruisers" would give chase, putting them under Kondo's big guns.

6. *Nagara* Action Report in *Tabular Records and Action Reports of Japanese Battleships and Cruisers.* Claims the sinking of "three enemy DDs."

7. *Combat Narratives*, vol. V, p. 60. The shore batteries were later discovered to be Japanese ships that had swung east of Savo Island.

8. *Combat Narratives*, vol. V, p. 64. The *Washington* quit firing at 1:02 A.M. because of an erroneous report that the target had sunk.

9. *Kirishima* Action Report in *Tabular Records and Action Reports of Japanese Battleships and Cruisers.*

10. *Nagara* Action Report. The *Nagara* acknowledged hits but also claimed the torpedoing of an "enemy BB." This is probably erroneous because no American battleship reported torpedo hits.

11. *Kirishima* Action Report.

12. Tanaka, pp. 191–94. This is the most authentic of all descriptions of the misfortunes of the transport convoy.

13. Ibid., pp. 193–96. Tanaka was certain the ships would be pounded to pieces. He was right.

14. *Combat Narratives*, vol. V, p. 68.

15. Roscoe, pp. 205–6.

# 14
# Death Struggle off Tassafaronga

**W**ashington was delighted with the naval victory at Guadalcanal. Navy Secretary Frank Knox told the press that now the Americans would defeat the Japanese. General Vandegrift praised Admirals Halsey, Scott, Callaghan, Kinkaid, and Lee. He declared that his marines would "raise their battered helmets in deepest admiration" for them. At Pearl, Admiral Nimitz praised Halsey, stating that he had that rare combination of intellectual and military audacity and could "calculate to a cat's whisker the risks involved." [1] For his part, Halsey praised the men of the navy for stopping the bombardment forces. But for the sacrifice of ships and men in Savo Sound, the Japanese would have wrecked Henderson Field and Tanaka's convoy "would have reached Guadalcanal with relative impunity." [2]

At Noumea, things were still hopping. Earlier, Halsey had gotten the Joint Chiefs of Staff to replace the ships lost around Guadalcanal, in spite of pressing demands in the Atlantic and North Africa. A new force of cruisers and destroyers had quickly appeared at Espiritu Santo and Noumea. Halsey then appointed Kinkaid to form this into Task Force 67, designed to derail Tanaka before he reached Guadalcanal.

Kinkaid had learned well from the battles. For him, there would be no single approach or unbroken column. He would use floatplanes to scout and drop flares when the enemy approach was spotted. His destroyers would dash in, launch torpedoes, and back off, allowing the cruisers to open fire at no less than 12,000 yards the minute the torpedoes struck home. Unlike the battle of Cape Esperance and the Guadalcanal engagements, the destroyers would have their most lethal advantage by operating independently.

The situation changed dramatically when, at the last minute, Kinkaid was sent to Alaska to relieve Adm. Robert A. Theobold, who was holding up a counteroffensive against the Japanese on Kiska. Nimitz was fed up with Theobold's constant dickering with the army. Adm. Carleton H. Wright was brought down from Pearl to take command of the task force. It was a poor choice because the worthy admiral was new to the area and was to command an untrained, hastily assembled unit.

Halsey had been studying reports of increased ship movements in the Shortlands and at Buin on the tip of Bougainville. This was ominous because it was thought that the enemy had left the troops on Guadalcanal twisting in the wind. By November 24, there were thirty Imperial ships where there had been twelve a week earlier. A large enemy attempt to reinforce his troops was imminent and this action had to be countered quickly. Task Force 67 was moved to Espiritu Santo and Wright and his commanders quickly discussed Kinkaid's plans. The force was to be divided into one destroyer and two cruiser units. Each was to be equipped with the new SC-1, a medium-range radar designed to detect surface ships and aircraft. The current SG radar was designed for surface craft alone; they were going to be used in tandem. Unit commanders were to assign a radar picket for continuous, all-around search. Contacts were to be reported by TBS to the unit commander, who would acknowledge the report.

The cruisers would form a line, with the destroyers in line to port to form a wedge. First contacts were to be made by radar. On contact, the destroyers were to attack with torpedoes. Then the smaller ships were to follow the cruisers in the attack and to send up star shells if ordered. The range was to be kept greater than 12,000 yards before the torpedo attack, then shellfire would commence at 10,000 to 12,000 yards with radar-directed fire control. Use of searchlights was forbidden and "fighting lights" were to be employed only if American ships were fired upon by friendlies.[3]

By all logic, the Japanese would have given up after losing the battleships *Hiei* and *Kirishima*, despite American losses of two heavy cruisers and seven destroyers. After all, destroyers could be replaced easily, but not capital ships. But Tanaka wouldn't be counted out. This warrior of the samurai tradition concluded that all was not lost. There would be another run down the Slot because the 10,000 Japanese on Guadalcanal were getting more desperate by the hour.

Since direct unloading from transports or destroyers onto barges was too dangerous and air drops were unworkable, Tanaka devised the drum method. Large metal drums or cans would be filled with medical supplies and food and then sealed, leaving enough air for buoyancy. The drums would be tied together and loaded onto destroyers. At the unloading point, the drums would be pushed overboard from the moving ship. A power boat from shore would pick up the end of the rope and tow the drums in. Submarines would also be used; they would surface at night, when U.S. planes were grounded, and push the drums overboard.

The idea was clever but inadequate. The troops were starving and supplies would be gone by the end of November. Tanaka had to make a major run now.

On November 27, he led his ships to anchor in the Shortlands, off Bougainville. His was the *Naganami,* a new 2,000-ton destroyer of the *Yagumo* class with five six-inch guns, eight twenty-four-inch torpedo tubes, and a streamlined bridge for less wind resistance. In her chart room, he described to his ship captains his plan for an eight-vessel run to Point Tassafaronga on Guadalcanal's northwest coast. He also updated them on the situation on the island. All knew that the enemy was wise to the Tokyo Express runs and would be out in force. American strength was growing around Guadalcanal but Imperial troops had to be supplied at all costs.

Two nights later, Tanaka weighed anchor. The *Naganami* was in the van, followed by the *Makanami,* the *Oyashio,* the *Kuroshio,* the *Kagero* (a new 2,000-tonner called the ultimate in Japanese destroyers), the *Kawakaze,* the *Suzukaze,* and the *Takanami.* He stationed the *Takanami* to port ahead in order to feel the way down the Slot. They sailed east for a while to throw off any enemy reconnaissance, then south.[4]

This fast-moving caravan was spotted by coast watchers, who flashed the word to the Americans at Tulagi. The warning was relayed to Halsey at Noumea. He moved fast, ordering Task Force 56, which had been on alert for twelve hours, to head north from Espiritu Santo at high speed. Wright had some fine ships in his force: the 10,000-ton heavy cruisers *Minneapolis* (the flagship), the *New Orleans,* the *Pensacola,* and the *Northampton;* the light cruiser *Honolulu;* and the destroyers *Fletcher, Perkins, Lamson, Maury, Drayton,* and *Lardner.* The 2,000-ton *Fletcher* ironically was the prototype of a new class built to answer the *Kagero*, with which it would shortly be bitterly engaged. The *Lamson* and the *Lardner* joined Wright at the last minute from an eastbound force of destroyers and transports. He made them the rear guard.

Early on the 30th, Wright advised his captains of the enemy's composition and of a possible night engagement. The destroyers were to steam two miles ahead of the *Minneapolis* before they entered the Lunga Channel. Then the destroyers were to take station and they, with the cruisers, would parallel the Guadalcanal coast by twelve miles. Any vessel seeing an enemy ship within 6,000 yards was to open fire immediately.

The night was murky but the sea was smooth as glass. The sweet smell of flowers mingled with the stink from the jungles of Guadalcanal. Wright's radars were smoothly sweeping the sound ahead and there would be no surprises tonight if he could help it. But the admiral had reason to worry a bit; he had taken over a task force at the last minute and the fleet wasn't well trained as a night-fighting unit. He knew too well the enemy's talent for fighting in the dark. He ordered the cruisers' planes, which had been launched earlier, to scout the sound. At first contact, they were to drop parachute flares.

Tanaka was also worried; his lookouts had reported the drone of planes overhead. Whether they were land-based seaplanes or carrier craft, they could mean trouble. He also was anxious because in order to carry the drums and troops, he had had to reduce ammunition for his ships and cut their number of torpedoes from sixteen to eight. Tanaka was relieved when he could steam down the Slot during the day unmolested, but there was always the chance American ships would pop up.

He didn't worry long. At 11:00 P.M., his lookouts sighted Guadalcanal's peak. Tassafaronga and the drop point were dead ahead. Speed was dropped to twelve knots and the column hugged the coast. Eight minutes later, a lookout reported unidentified ships ahead. His night binoculars had picked up a formation of seven destroyers (actually, they were the four ships of Wright's van). A hissing pop was heard and a parachute flare blossomed in the black sky, lighting everything in a wide circle beneath it.[5] Tanaka spotted the *Takanami*, off to port, in the light. He halted the unloading and got ready to fight.

A radar man on the *Minneapolis* discovered Tanaka's column at a range of 23,000 yards, making fifteen knots. The radar man reported the contact as being "like a small wart on Cape Esperance." The "wart" soon became detached from the land mass and formed a column of seven ships. At 11:08 P.M., Wright turned left, putting the cruisers in the center with the van destroyers on his starboard flank and the rear guard on his port flank. Fifteen minutes later, he ordered another turn, and the two forces were speeding toward each other on reversed parallel courses.

Then a *Fletcher* radar man picked up two targets, 14,000 yards off her port bow, followed by five ships a quarter-mile off Guadalcanal. Another contact was made a mile abreast of the column. The skipper, Comdr. William M. Cole, asked to launch torpedoes. Wright was worried about the range and hesitated. By the time he gave permission, Tanaka's ships had slipped by the *Fletcher*'s port quarter. The *Fletcher* launched her fish, but the spread was lost, but not to Tanaka's lookouts. They raised the alarm.

Wright's cruisers opened fire. The *Perkins* launched torpedoes to no effect, star shells were flung aloft, and the battle was opened with considerable confusion that doomed the *Takanami*. She had fired her torpedoes and made a sharp right turn that exposed her flank to the Americans. Most of Wright's ships concentrated on the destroyer because she was the closest. She was battered beyond recognition and burning.[6] Remarkably, this tough ship sent off a cutterload of soldiers before she died.

The *Takanami*'s bonfire gave Tanaka's crews a shield behind which to spring into action. He ordered a 180-degree turn that put his ships parallel to the enemy's. Spread after spread of Long Lances sped toward the American ships. In spite of decks cluttered with freight, Tanaka's crews launched close to fifty torpedoes, all because of a bit of hesitation!

The *Naganami* pinned an American cruiser in her searchlight and opened fire. She then turned hard about and ran parallel with the

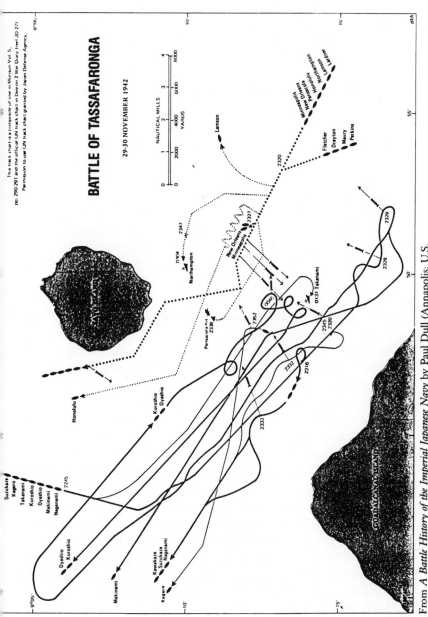

# BATTLE OF TASSAFARONGA

## 29-30 NOVEMBER 1942

This track chart is a composite of one in *Morison* Vol. 5, pp. 290-291 and the official IJN track chart in *Detron 2 War Diary* (reel JD 27). Permission to use IJN track chart granted by Japan Defense Agency.

From *A Battle History of the Imperial Japanese Navy* by Paul Dull (Annapolis: U.S. Naval Institute, 1978).

enemy. She launched eight torpedoes while taking numerous shell hits. Meanwhile, her sisters, the *Oyashio*, the *Kuroshio*, and the *Kawa-kaze*, were busy flinging torpedoes. Moments later, a Japanese captain reported an enemy cruiser hit, set afire, and sinking. The *Kagero* was busy with her powerful searchlights, spotting ships and hammering away. The rest of Tanaka's ships were swinging into action.

Tanaka later said he felt the American column had been thrown into confusion. Other ships, reported as enemy destroyers, were seen being hit and set ablaze. His torpedoes gone, it was time to withdraw. He was anxious about the *Takanami* and repeated calls to her went unanswered. The *Oyashio* and the *Kuroshio* found her east of Cape Esperance, crippled and motionless. The *Oyashio* had lowered life-boats and the *Kuroshio* had come alongside when American ships, reported as two cruisers and three destroyers, appeared at close range. The Japanese had to leave the *Takanami* survivors to their own devices. Many did make the shore of Guadalcanal.

Tanaka was right; the Americans were confused. The *Fletcher* had been forced to waste torpedo shots. Meanwhile, the *Minneapolis* had picked up a target to the right of the enemy column and reported it as a transport. The first salvos went over, but the next three hit. The ship was reported to have disintegrated.[7] Gunfire and star shells were flying everywhere, and then there were all those Long Lances.

The *Minneapolis* was the first to be hit. At 11:27 P.M., a torpedo hit forward of turret No. 2, abreast of the aviation fuel compartment, and a second hit in the No. 2 fireroom. Flames shot skyward and the bow section tore off, folded under, and dangled from the hull. Fire-rooms 1, 2, and 3 flooded, causing many casualties. Still, she kept firing, one of her shells barely missing the *Pensacola* maneuvering to port.

When the *Minneapolis* was torpedoed, the *New Orleans*, next in line, swung right to avoid a collision and ran into a Long Lance that sheared off her bow up to the No. 2 turret. The bow floated aft along the port side, tearing holes in the hull. At 11:39, the *Pensacola* was silhouetted by the burning ships and took a torpedo on the port side aft, just forward of turret No. 3, igniting fuel tanks. She became a blazing wreck and limped off toward Tulagi.

The Long Lances had spread out like sharks and found still another target, the *Northampton*, maneuvering wildly to avoid her wounded sisters and the oncoming fish. She was hit twice at the waterline, igniting fuel and diesel oil and spraying flames over the superstructure and boat deck. The latter contained five-inch shells that exploded, adding to the carnage. Then the port side blew out, leaving her listing twenty degrees to port. Skipper Frank L. Lowe ordered her abandoned. She rolled over and sank at 3:00 A.M.

By now, ships of both sides were scattered. After their initial torpedo run, Wright's van destroyers had, according to plan, swung up and around Savo Island. They entered the sound again at 12:07 A.M. to find the American column shattered. Now their task was to pick up survivors. The rear-guard *Lamson* and *Lardner*, too far astern to participate in the action, helped in the rescue. The *Minneapolis*, the *New Orleans*, and the *Pensacola* crawled off toward Tulagi, where they were moored and camouflaged.

Tanaka realized that he had inflicted heavy damage and that searching for the *Takanami*'s survivors was too dangerous, so at 1:30 A.M., the Tokyo Express roared up the Slot for the Shortlands. He had sunk a heavy cruiser and put three more out of commission for months, at the loss of one destroyer. Though it was a tactical victory for him, he had again lost a round to the Americans because he hadn't unloaded all of his cargo and men on Guadalcanal. But Tanaka had shattered the American countereffort. He lamented that he couldn't pick up survivors of the *Takanami*, but he was unsure how many enemy ships were left in the sound and, of course, his ships were out of torpedoes. Here, discretion was the better part of valor.

This man, who had conducted a most difficult task and suffered heavy losses in the process, would successfully evacuate troops from Guadalcanal, only to be relieved of sea command and given a desk job in December. It is odd that no one in General Headquarters said, "Would that we had more commanders like Tanaka." Such was the strange thinking of Japan's leaders during the war. Perhaps they were trying to cover up their own blunders by passing on the blame to men who dutifully carried out faulty orders. Who knows? After the war, only a few Imperial officers attempted to place blame where it belonged.

The American Navy, on the other hand, promoted officers who showed skill, determination, and tenacity, and blame was often placed where it belonged.

This savage thirty-minute conflict pointed out some defects in American strategy and execution: lack of training in night battle, inability of radar to distinguish enemy ships from the coastlines, ineffective use of floatplanes, and the lack of flashless powder, which allowed Tanaka's crews to home in on our ships. Most critical was the poor coordination among commanders and a complete lack of indoctrination because of the haste in which the force was put together. The *Lamson* and *Lardner* were never put to full use because the timing prevented their skippers from receiving operational plans. By the time they were brought up, the battle was over. They might have altered the outcome. And don't forget Admiral Wright's hesitation over the *Fletcher*'s request for action.

All of this is hindsight and no one really knows what effect these factors had against an enemy highly efficient in night battle and torpedo tactics. It was apparent that much work had yet to be done by the navy. Happily, it was done, as Operation Cartwheel—the planned climb up the Slot toward Rabaul—proved in a few months. But that's another story.

If you are tempted to shake your head over Wright's defeat, imagine what it was like to fight a naval battle at close quarters and in pitch darkness. Remember that the vaunted U.S. radar at that time couldn't distinguish between friend and foe and that the Japanese were great night fighters. I wasn't in this particular battle, but I was in others. Here's what it was like.

You're steaming along in the Slot (or any other body of water) toward what you know will be a battle area and your whole universe is concentrated on your ship. The only sounds are the hissing of water past the hull, the muted throbbing of the ship's turbines, and an occasional nervous whisper from a shipmate. You know the enemy is out there and when you meet, no quarter will be given. Your eyes strain to penetrate the darkness until they ache, even though you know that the radar is on the job; you're hoping you spot the enemy first. Your heart pounds so loudly that you're afraid it will betray your ship's position. Your hands grip your gun handles or splinter shield until knuckles are white. Your mouth is dry and you long for a tall, cold drink.

Suddenly, the darkness is split by an orange-white flash followed by a flat-sounding BLAAAP! A streamer of light reaches out for your ship. Your heart seems to stop beating and you realize that you've been holding your breath. There's another flash and another. Tracers arc across the sky, coming your way. The enemy has found you first and there's hell to pay. You ask, "Why didn't radar pick them up first? What happened?" But there's no time for questions.

Your ship lurches to one side as the helmsman swings her out of range of those missiles. Then the fire control people get the range. Orders come over the ship's phone to your gun captain: "range . . . elevation . . . commence firing!" Your gun barks out and you're blinded by the flash because your eyes had been accustomed to darkness. Your face is whipped hard by the concussion and you choke on the powder fumes. Then you go into a trance—everything is automatic. You load and fire, load and fire, until your fear is temporarily checked by the task at hand.

The black universe has been ripped apart. The horizon becomes a kaleidoscope of gun flashes; star shells hang in the sky, bathing everything in a ghostly light; incandescent tracers crisscross the sky; the air is filled with the heavy, rolling thunder of gunfire; an occasional, brilliant, white-hot flash marks a ship blowing up and you silently pray it isn't one of yours. You go on firing.

Then there's a heavy thump. A geyser of water rises alongside and you instinctively duck. A near-miss! Sometimes you're sprayed with water, but you shake it off, thankful it wasn't a direct hit. It could have been a torpedo slamming into the side.

Through your earphones, you hear, "Ship off port bow!" Everyone strains to get a look. There it is! Silhouetted by flashes and burning hulls is a destroyer. Is it ours or the enemy's? If it's ours, what's she doing in our line of fire? If the enemy's, why is she so close? You're told to stop firing for fear of hitting one of our own. You watch as the dark shape slips by. If it were the enemy, he was as surprised as we. Close call!

Everyone is worried about those Long Lances we've heard so much about. No wake. They just sneak up on you.

By this time, your universe is reverberating from the deafening rumble of gunfire and, if you're smart, you've stuffed cotton in your ears. At least no one will hear your wildly beating heart!

When it's finally over and your ship is undamaged, the numbness leaves and fear returns. You shiver from the trauma and often a coldness sets in. You wish someone would put a blanket around your body.

All this is why things get confused during ship-to-ship combat; it's a mad dance of death. Sometimes, such as at the first battle of Guadalcanal, it becomes a melee with every man for himself. Sometimes the ships get so close that the crews fire at each other with handguns. They did at the first battle of Guadalcanal.

At Tassafaronga, as in other battles, the U.S. Navy hadn't properly reckoned with Admiral Tanaka, though the Americans considered him one of Japan's most brilliant tacticians, one who could outsmart and outfight U.S. forces again and again. But Tanaka was fighting a losing battle of his own. He didn't know that his high command had decided to evacuate Guadalcanal, and he was left to fight for his life while trying to supply those forces.

Tassafaronga was the last sea battle for control of Guadalcanal and the southeastern Pacific. Never again did Yamamoto commit transports and heavy units to the area. Everything was left up to Tanaka and his overworked destroyers, which could only manage a trickle of reinforcements and supplies. Wright's three crippled cruisers were hidden in coves at Tulagi while emergency repairs were made. The *Pensacola* eventually went to Pearl Harbor and the *Minneapolis* to Espiritu Santo and then to Pearl. The *New Orleans* made it safely to

Sydney, Australia, limping along at six to seven knots. Fortunately, no enemy subs were about. Once again, the United States was dangerously low on ships in the southeastern Pacific, but not for long. The brass had put a high priority on the Solomons and Operation Cartwheel was soon to be launched.

## NOTES

1. Potter, *Nimitz*, p. 208.

2. Potter, *Bull Halsey*, p. 186.

3. *Combat Narratives*, vol. VII, pp. 197–99.

4. Tanaka, pp. 197–99. He was fully expecting surface action and was not taken by surprise, as some have written.

5. Tanaka, p. 200. The fact that planes were heard by his lookouts and that a flare had been dropped would contradict Morison and *Combat Narratives*, since Wright's scout planes didn't get airborne until after the battle.

6. *Combat Narratives*, vol. VII, pp. 9–10. The battle reports of U.S. ships claimed hits on enemy ships. Each report concluded a ship was sunk. Actually, all were firing at the *Takanami* because she was alone and to the port of Tanaka's column.

7. Ibid., pp. 11–13. Some of Wright's captains reported a *Yubari*- or *Mogami*-type cruiser, plus a transport and a cargo ship. There were no such Japanese ships present.

## 15
# End of the Line
# for the Tokyo Express

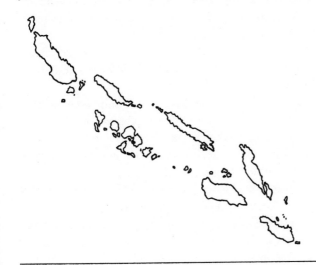

On November 31, the day after the battle of Tassafaronga, Imperial headquarters decided to give up trying to occupy Guadalcanal. The situation had become so intolerable that it refused to expend any more precious men or ships there. The thick Japanese heads had finally been penetrated. KE Operation would withdraw troops from the island by way of Cape Esperance on February 2–3, 4–5, and 7–8, using all available destroyers, submarines, planes, and transports. After the evacuation, according to the plan, a new air base would be established at Munda Point on New Georgia. The work was to be done under the camouflage of a coconut grove.

KE Operation required many ships in Rabaul and Buin. Thirteen destroyers were allocated to Tanaka for his Tokyo Express runs so the 25,000 troops could be supplied until KE was launched. Tanaka plunged into the task with his usual energy. On December 3, he made the first run with ten destroyers; on the 7th, the first anniversary of Pearl Harbor, eleven destroyers made a night run. As he approached Cape Esperance, PT boats torpedoed one of his ships, damaging her so badly she had to be towed back to base.

On December 11, his ships were again attacked in the Slot. Tanaka was slightly wounded and his flagship, the new 2,500-ton *Teruzuki*, was sunk near Kolombangora. After a few days of recuperation, he was back on the bridge of his new flagship, the *Naganami*. But time was running out for Tenacious Tanaka. After one more run on December 15, he returned to Rabaul. He was relieved of all sea duties on the 19th and sent home for a much-deserved rest. Rear Adm. Tomiji Koyanagi took over his command.

In the meantime, KE Operation had started. Ships were divided between Rabaul and the Shortlands for the evacuation of troops. Plans were hastily changed when some transports and two heavy cruisers were damaged during B-17 raids on Rabaul. Headquarters decided to put the burden of the evacuation on the shoulders of Koyanagi and his destroyers. To counter any ambitious resistance to KE, the Combined Fleet stationed the carriers *Zuikaku*, *Zuibo*, and *Junyo*; six heavy cruisers; two light cruisers; and eleven destroyers north of the Solomons. They were to intervene only if the Americans brought up heavy naval units.

Almost 5,000 men were evacuated on the night of February 2–3 despite an ineffectual PT boat attack. However, the destroyer *Makigumo* hit a mine off Savo Island and was lost. On February 4–5, the Japanese evacuated 3,921 soldiers, though a destroyer was damaged during an air attack. The final run on February 7–8 removed about 1,800 men from Guadalcanal and Russell islands. One destroyer was damaged.

The Japanese had recovered a third of their original 31,358-man force from Guadalcanal. The Americans were stunned. They thought the destroyer runs were only reinforcement attempts, so they didn't do much to stop them. No U.S. fleet units were called up. In fact, U.S. forces on Guadalcanal didn't know that the Japanese had left until February 9, when they made an end-run landing on Cape Esperance and found it deserted.

The Japanese evacuation ended the struggle for the southeastern Solomons. The battles from August 7, 1942, through February 17, 1943, had cost the Imperial Navy a carrier, two battleships, four cruisers, and ten destroyers. The Americans lost two carriers, seven cruisers, and twenty-one destroyers. The price had been dreadful, but the effects were long-range: the Japanese had been thrown back to an upper defense line that in the months to come would be rolled back farther and farther until they were forced out of the Solomons. The Americans counted it as a major victory. Australia and her supply lines were no longer threatened and Guadalcanal became a strong base from which to climb up the Solomons toward Tokyo itself.

The Tokyo Express faded into history.

Evidence gathered since 1942–43 has clearly shown that the loss of Guadalcanal was the beginning of the end for Japan. Although the battle of Midway set back Imperial expansion, the Japanese did take Kiska in the western Aleutians and establish a base there. Meanwhile, the warlords sought to occupy New Britain and march over the Owen Stanley Mountains of New Guinea to assault Port Moresby. And Imperial headquarters was casting eyes toward Guadalcanal and the Russell Islands in the southeastern Pacific.

Yamamoto still commanded forces twice the size of the U.S. Navy. His Combined Fleet was rigorously trained and, in spite of the loss of four fleet carriers and their seasoned pilots, he could muster six flattops. More were being built or converted. The rest of Yamamoto's surface forces were intact and included the two largest battleships in the world, the *Yamato* and the *Musashi*, with their eighteen-inch guns. Small wonder that the Japanese continued with their southeastern Pacific plans!

The problem is that they overreached in the Solomons. After the war, Rear Adm. Masanori Ito wrote that Japan had exceeded its "offensive terminal point," after which an army's strength diminishes. In other words, the offensive terminal point lies just before the tide of battle would turn. It is the ideal time for the offensive force to hold, rest, and strengthen its lines of communication, supply, and reinforcement before taking the next step. Ito stated Japan's terminal point should have been the East Indies and Borneo, consolidating them and protecting the flow of oil and minerals to the homeland. He concluded that the fault lay with General Headquarters.

"It is now clear," he maintained, "that Japan went to war totally ignoring from the outset the offensive terminal point." Even Rabaul, he decided, was beyond it.[1]

Therefore, to continue operations in the Solomons, the Combined Fleet had to commit ships piecemeal in order to reinforce Guadalcanal. It cost twenty-four warships, 893 planes with 2,362 airmen, and 16,000 troops. Those losses couldn't be replaced, whereas American industries could more than keep up with losses.

Another of Japan's warriors, Rear Adm. Yoshiyuki Yokai, wrote: "the fall of Guadalcanal in February of 1943 was the turning point in the Pacific war. Japan's naval offensive strategy was forced on the defensive." He blamed the outdated "battleship doctrines" of obstinate leaders.[2]

Naval historians put much of the blame on Yamamoto. While his destroyers were being decimated in the Solomons, he kept his big ships at Truk. He seemed reluctant to commit massive power to the area, though he said he badly wanted a decisive engagement with the Americans. Had he committed the Combined Fleet to the area after the American landings on Guadalcanal in August 1942 or in the battle of the Eastern Solomons the same month, at Santa Cruz in

October, or even in the Guadalcanal sea battles in November, he might have driven the Americans out of the Solomons.

Did he know that at one point in October, the U.S. Navy was down to one operational carrier? Did he not know that Halsey's forces, like those of Ghormley before him, were always numerically inferior to his? There was an unexplainable weakness in his intelligence. Perhaps Yamamoto was still shaken over Midway. His reasons died with him over Bougainville in April 1943.[3]

The man who bore the brunt of the fighting on the Japanese side was Tanaka. More than once he met, fought, and defeated American forces with his limited complement of destroyers. He showed the Americans the techniques of torpedo tactics and night fighting. He was a man who would never run from a fight, even if the adversary was numerically and technologically superior. But Tanaka was fighting a losing battle of his own. Unknown to him, the Japanese brass had already decided to evacuate Guadalcanal, and he was left to fight lost causes, attempting to supply garrisons that were already marked for evacuation.

Tanaka survived the war. In his declining years, he wrote about his Tokyo Express and its defeat. He gave these problems he was up against: 1. Confusion in command. More than once, he was subject to orders from three commands and often instructions were conflicting and incompatible. 2. Hastily gathered forces in which crews and commanders had no opportunity to practice or operate together. 3. There were no consistent operational plans. Ships and men were put together piecemeal for an operation without long-range planning. 4. Poor communications. 5. Lack of coordination between the army and navy. Each branch made independent plans without regard for the other. 6. Underestimation of the enemy. The enemy's successes were belittled while the Japanese high command inflated its own capabilities and victories. 7. Inferiority in the air. Time and again, Tanaka had to run down the Slot without air cover. This recklessness, he maintained, resulted in a dreadful loss of ships and men. He said, "We stumbled along from one error to another, while the enemy grew wise."[4]

But Raizo Tanaka had done his job. He retired with dignity and died peacefully on his little farm in 1959.

The Americans did "grow wise," as Tanaka said. The U.S. Navy learned many lessons from the fighting around Guadalcanal. First, a crash effort was made to train crews in night fighting. This was also important considering the relative impotence of radar in confined waters such as the Solomons. Until radar was refined in early 1943, it was frustrating when enemy ships hugged the coast, as Tanaka did so effectively in the battle of Tassafaronga.

The use of the battle line was declared outdated in the face of an enemy that would turn his destroyers loose to use their most potent weapon, the torpedo. When Admiral Scott countermarched at Cape Esperance, he kept his destroyers in line; they could not use one bank of their torpedo tubes or the full radius of their guns. The U.S. Navy changed the rule books, as battles up the Slot in 1943 showed.

Poor communications among ships and with aircraft plagued American forces. The indiscriminate use of TBS and frequencies resulted in hubbubs that prevented commanders from directing the battles, as seen at the Eastern Solomons, Santa Cruz, and the battles of Guadalcanal. Later communications were tightly controlled by technical improvements and strict rules governing use.

Perhaps the greatest failings of U.S. forces were their faulty torpedoes and firing tactics. In many instances, U.S. torpedo spreads were totally ineffective. The twenty-one-inch gas turbine-propelled torpedoes compared poorly with the magnificent oxygen-propelled Long Lances. Part of the problem was because of parsimony. As a former destroyerman, I can recall many instances when we would fire torpedoes in practice and were then ordered to recover them if possible because they were expensive. The Japanese freely expended torpedoes in order to hone their techniques. This deficiency also was eventually remedied and the U.S. Navy gave a good account of itself with torpedoes for the rest of the war.

Hastily gathered task forces without tactical unit training also were a problem for the Americans. This is understandable, considering the few ships allocated to Ghormley and Halsey. They had to

# Naval ship losses during the struggle for Guadalcanal

## ALLIED

**Battleships:** None
**Carriers:** *Hornet, Wasp*
**Cruisers:** *Vincennes, Quincy, Astoria, Canberra* (Australian), *Atlanta, Juneau,* and *Northampton*
**Destroyers:** *Duncan, Cushing, Laffey, Barton, Monssen, Walke, Preston, Benham, Blue, Jarvis, Meredith,* and *O'Brien*

## JAPANESE

**Battleships:** *Hiei, Kirishima*
**Carrier:** *Ryujo*
**Cruisers:** *Furutaka, Kinusaga, Kako,* and *Yura*
**Destroyers:** *Asagumo, Asagiri, Murakumo, Terutzuki, Michishio, Fubuki, Akatsuki, Yudachi, Ayanami,* and *Takanami*
**Transports:** Eleven

make good with what they had, in light of European priorities. This too was corrected when future task forces and battle groups were rigorously trained together.

Thus the loss of Guadalcanal was the strategic turning point for Japan in the war. As Paul Dull stated in *Battle History of the Imperial Japanese Navy,* "Guadalcanal and the later fall of New Guinea was the turning point, for there would be no more Japanese advances. Japan had overreached herself with disastrous results." [5]

Even Tanaka said, "There is no question that Japan's doom was sealed with the closing struggle for Guadalcanal."[6] After the war, Rear Adm. Sokichi Takagi of the Naval General Staff admitted that when the Allies invaded the Solomons, he said to himself that if Japan lost there, "all roads would lead to Tokyo."[7]

History was to show that, during 1943, the Japanese retreated up the Solomons ladder until they were driven out completely, falling back on their bases in the Admiralty Islands (which were to become one of the most important staging points for U.S. forces in the final fifteen months of the war); the islands of Palau, Yap, and Ulithi; and the Philippines, all part of a gigantic dagger aimed at the heart of the empire. In the ensuing months of 1943 and 1944, those islands were taken by a combined Central Pacific and southeastern Pacific drive, and the dagger was finally driven home.

## NOTES

1. Masanori Ito, *The End of the Imperial Japanese Navy* (New York: McFadden-Bartell, 1965), pp. 69–71.

2. Toshiyuki Yokoi, "Thoughts on Japan's Naval Defeat," in Evans, pp. 514–15.

3. Burke Davis, *Get Yamamoto* (New York: Random House, 1969). Includes an extensive account of the death of Yamamoto, an authoritative description of the breaking of the JN-25 code, and the interception of his air convoy in the Solomons.

4. Tanaka, pp. 209–11.

5. Dull, p. 260.

6. Tanaka, p. 211.

7. R. J. Butow, *Japan's Decision to Surrender* (Stanford, Calif.: Stanford University Press, 1954). This profound work delves into the military and political squabbles that inexorably led to Japan's defeat. It is highly recommended to the student of the Pacific war.

# Bibliography

## NAVAL PUBLICATIONS

The bulk of research was done at the Operational Archives Branch, Navy Historical Division, Navy Yard, Washington, D.C.

*Combat Narratives*, Vols. II–VIII. Washington, D.C.: Office of Naval Intelligence, 1944–45. Microfilm.

*Interrogation of Japanese Officials*. 2 Vols. Washington, D.C.: United States Strategic Bombing Survey, Naval Analysis Division, 1945.

*Tabular Records and Action Reports of Japanese Battleships and Cruisers*, (TJ-1), Washington, D.C.: Operational Archives Branch, U.S. Navy Historical Center. Microfilm.

## BOOKS

Agawa, Hiroyuki, trans. John Bester. *The Reluctant Admiral: Yamamoto and the Imperial Navy.* Tokyo: Kodansha International Ltd., 1979.

Barck, Oscar Theodore Jr., and Nelson Manfred Blake. *Since 1900: A History of the United States in Our Times.* New York: Macmillan Co., 1952.

Butow, R. J. *Japan's Decision to Surrender.* Stanford, Calif.: Stanford University Press, 1954.

Calvocoress, Peter, Guy Wint and John Pritchard. *Total War: Causes and Courses of the Second World War.* New York: Pantheon Books, 1987.

Cook, Charles. *The Battle of Cape Esperance.* New York: Thomas Y. Crowell, 1968.

Davis, Burke. *Get Yamamoto.* New York: Random House, 1969.

Dean, John. *Yamamoto.* New York: Viking Press, 1965.

Dulin, Robert O., and William H. Garske Jr. *Battleships: U.S. Battleships in World War II.* Annapolis: Naval Institute Press, 1976.

Dull, Paul S. *A Battle History of the Imperial Japanese Navy: 1941–45.* Annapolis: Naval Institute Press, 1978.

Evans, David C., ed. *The Japanese Navy in World War II in the Words of Former Japanese Naval Officers.* Annapolis: Naval Institute Press, 1986.

Fahey, James C. *The Ships and Aircraft of the U.S. Fleet.* New York: Gemso Inc., 1944.

Fitzimmons, Bernard, ed. *Warships of the Second World War.* Leicester, England: Anster, 1972.

Fuchida, Mitsuo, and Masatake Okumiya. *Midway: The Battle That Doomed Japan.* New York: Ballantine Books, 1955.

Goodenough, Simon. *War Maps, World War II, from September 1939 to August 1945, Air, Sea, and Land, Battle by Battle.* New York: St. Martin's Press, 1982.

Hammel, Eric. *Guadalcanal: The Carrier Battles.* New York: Crown Publishers Inc., 1987.

———. *Guadalcanal: Decision at Sea, the Naval Battles of Guadalcanal, Nov. 13–15, 1942.* New York: Crown Publishers Inc., 1988.

Hamilton, John. *War at Sea, 1939–1945.* New York: Blandford Press, 1986.

Hara, Tomeichi, with Fred Saito and Roger Pineau. *Japanese Destroyer Captain.* New York: Ballantine Books, 1961.

Hoyt, Edwin P. *How They Won the War in the Pacific: Nimitz and His Admirals.* New York: Weybright and Talley, 1970.

———. *Japan's War: The Great Pacific Conflict.* New York: McGraw-Hill, 1986.

————. *Yamamoto, the Man Who Planned Pearl Harbor.* New York: McGraw-Hill, 1990.

Ito, Masanori, with Roger Pineau. *The End of the Imperial Japanese Navy.* New York: McFadden-Bartell, 1965.

Jacobsen, Hans-Adolph, and Arthur L. Smith, Jr. *World War II Policy and Strategy: Selected Documents with Commentary.* Claremont, Calif.: Regina Books, 1979.

Karig, Walter, and Eric Purdon. *Battle Report, Pacific War,* 5 Vols., *Middle Phase,* Vol. 3. New York: Rinehart and Co. Inc., 1947.

Keegan, John, and Andrew Wheatcroft. *Who's Who in Military History.* New York: William Morrow and Co. Inc., 1976.

McDonald, John. *Great Battles of World War II.* New York: Macmillan, 1986.

Mayer, Edward S. L. *The Japanese War Machine.* New Jersey: Chartwell Books, 1976.

Merillat, H. B. *Guadalcanal Remembered.* New York: Dodd, Mead, and Co., 1982.

Miller, John Jr. *Cartwheel: The Reduction of Rabaul.* Washington, D.C.: Department of the Army, U.S. Government Printing Office, 1959.

Morison, Samuel E. *History of United States Naval Operations in World War II,* Vol. 5, "The Struggle for Guadalcanal," Boston: Little, Brown and Co., 1949.

————. *The Two-Ocean War: A Short History of the U.S. Navy in the Second World War.* Boston: Little, Brown and Co., 1963.

Newcomb, Richard F. *Savo.* New York: Bantam Books, 1961.

Okumiya, Masatake, and Horoshiki Jiro. *Zero.* New York: Ballantine Books, 1956.

Potter, E. B. *Bull Halsey.* Annapolis: Naval Institute Press, 1985.

————. *Nimitz.* Annapolis: Naval Institute Press, 1976.

Potter, John Dean. *Yamamoto.* New York: Viking Press, 1965.

Prange, Gordon. *Miracle at Midway.* New York: McGraw-Hill, 1982.

*Reports of General MacArthur, Japanese Operations in the Southwest Pacific Area,* Vol. II. Washington, D.C.: U.S. Government Printing Office, 1966.

Roscoe, Theodore. *U.S. Destroyer Operations in World War II*. Annapolis: Naval Institute Press, 1953.

Silverstone, Paul H. *U.S. Warships of World War II*. Annapolis: U.S. Naval Institute Press, 1989.

Spector, Ronald H. *Eagle Against the Sun – The American War with Japan*. New York: Free Press, 1985.

Stafford, Edward P. *The Big E: The Story of the USS Enterprise*. New York: Random House, 1962.

Tillman, Barrett. *The Dauntless Dive Bomber of World War II*. Annapolis: Naval Institute Press, 1976.

Tregaskis, Richard. *Guadalcanal Diary*. New York: Random House, 1943.

Tuleja, Thaddeus. *Climax at Midway*. New York: Berkeley Publishing Corp., 1961.

Watts, Anthony J., and Brian G. Gordon. *The Imperial Japanese Navy*. New York: Doubleday & Co. Inc., 1971.

## PRIVATELY PRINTED SOURCES

Muehrcke, Robert C., ed. *Orchids in the Mud: Personal Accounts by Veterans of the 132nd Infantry Regiment*. Chicago: 132nd Infantry Regiment of World War II Association, 1985.

*The True Story of BB57, USS South Dakota, the Queen of the Fleet*. Dallas: BB57 Book Committee, Taylor Publishing Co., 1987.

# Index